First World War
and Army of Occupation
War Diary
France, Belgium and Germany

9 DIVISION
South African Brigade
1 South African Infantry Regiment
4 March 1916 - 28 February 1918

WO95/1780

The Naval & Military Press Ltd
www.nmarchive.com
Published in association with The National Archives

Published by

The Naval & Military Press Ltd

Unit 10 Ridgewood Industrial Park,

Uckfield, East Sussex,

TN22 5QE England

Tel: +44 (0) 1825 749494

www.naval-military-press.com

www.nmarchive.com

This diary has been reprinted in facsimile from the original. Any imperfections are inevitably reproduced and the quality may fall short of modern type and cartographic standards.

© Crown Copyright
Images reproduced by permission of The National Archives, London, England, 2015.

Contents

Document type	Place/Title	Date From	Date To
Heading	9th Scottish Division 5th African Infy Bde. 1st 5th African Infy Regt. Jun-Dec 1916 Diaries For Apr & May 1916 Are Missing.		
Heading	1st South African Infantry Regiment.		
Operation(al) Order(s)	Map. Trench Man 36. M.W.2. 1/10,000. 1st South African Infantry Brigade Operation Order No. 26 App 114	13/05/1916	13/05/1916
War Diary		01/06/1916	01/07/1916
War Diary	Trigger Wood.	02/07/1916	03/07/1916
War Diary	German 1st Syston	04/03/1916	04/03/1916
War Diary	Montauban Maricourt	05/07/1916	07/07/1916
War Diary	Brikol Old	08/07/1916	08/07/1916
War Diary	1st Line Trenches	09/07/1916	09/07/1916
War Diary	Maricourt.	10/07/1916	12/07/1916
War Diary	Samer	13/07/1916	14/07/1916
War Diary	Longueval	14/07/1916	31/07/1916
Map			
War Diary	Frevillers	01/08/1916	10/08/1916
War Diary	Villers au Bois	18/08/1916	22/08/1916
War Diary	Sapport Line Berthonval	23/08/1916	24/08/1916
War Diary	Frevillers	10/08/1916	14/08/1916
War Diary	Villers Au Bois	16/08/1916	17/08/1916
Map			
War Diary	Berthonval II	31/08/1916	31/08/1916
War Diary	Support Line Berthonval	25/08/1916	31/08/1916
War Diary	Support Line Berthonval	01/09/1916	03/09/1916
War Diary	Maisnil Bouche	04/09/1916	05/09/1916
War Diary	Front Line Carency. II	06/09/1916	17/09/1916
War Diary	Villers au Bois	18/09/1916	20/09/1916
War Diary	Carency II Front Line	21/09/1916	22/09/1916
War Diary	Camblain L'Abbe	23/09/1916	23/09/1916
War Diary	Berthonsart	24/09/1916	24/09/1916
War Diary	Maizieres	25/09/1916	28/09/1916
War Diary	Grand Rulle Court	29/09/1916	05/10/1916
War Diary	Bonnieres	06/10/1916	06/10/1916
War Diary	Lahoussoye	07/10/1916	07/10/1916
War Diary	Mametz Wood	08/10/1916	08/10/1916
War Diary	Bazentin Legrand	09/10/1916	10/10/1916
War Diary	Millencourt	25/10/1916	27/10/1916
War Diary	Duisans	29/10/1916	31/10/1916
War Diary	Rebempre	28/10/1916	28/10/1916
War Diary	Bazentin Le Grand	11/10/1916	11/10/1916
War Diary	High Wood	12/10/1916	12/10/1916
War Diary	Star Fish Trench	13/10/1916	16/10/1916
War Diary	Front Line Eaucourt L'Abbe	17/10/1916	19/10/1916
War Diary	High Wood	20/10/1916	20/10/1916
War Diary	Bazentin Le Grand	21/10/1916	22/10/1916
War Diary	Mametz Wood	23/10/1916	23/10/1916
War Diary	Albert	24/10/1916	24/10/1916

Miscellaneous	Sab. Conf. 15/0. 1st South African Infantry Regiment. 24th October 1916	24/10/1916	24/10/1916
Operation(al) Order(s)	Provisional Operation Orders.	22/10/1916	22/10/1916
Map			
Map	SAI Brigade Sketch Map		
War Diary	Duisans	01/11/1916	30/11/1916
War Diary	Duisans	01/12/1916	02/12/1916
War Diary	Front Line Arras Sub Section J.I	03/12/1916	31/12/1916
War Diary	Front Line Arras-J.I. Sub Section	20/12/1916	22/12/1916
War Diary	Arras	23/12/1916	29/12/1916
Heading	9th Scottish Division South African Infy Bde. 1st Sth African Infy Regt Jan-Dec 1917		
Heading	9th Division S.A. Infy Brigade S.A. Infy 1917		
War Diary	Arras Front Line J.I. Sub. Section	01/01/1917	16/01/1917
War Diary	Arras	23/01/1917	31/01/1917
War Diary	Arras Front Line J.I. Sub. Section	17/01/1917	23/01/1917
War Diary	Sub Section Arras Front Line	01/02/1917	13/02/1917
War Diary	J-I Section Rt. Sector Arras Front Line	14/02/1917	17/02/1917
War Diary	Arras Support Line	16/02/1917	25/02/1917
War Diary	No. 1 Section R.t. Sector Front Line Arras	26/02/1917	27/02/1917
War Diary	No.1 Section	28/02/1917	28/02/1917
War Diary	Front Line Arras No.1 Sect. Rt. Sector	01/03/1917	03/03/1917
War Diary	Y. Hutments W-Etrun	04/03/1917	11/03/1917
War Diary	Monchy-Breton	12/03/1917	21/03/1917
War Diary	Hermaville	22/03/1917	23/03/1917
War Diary	Penin	24/03/1917	31/03/1917
War Diary	Yhutments Near Etrun	01/04/1917	02/04/1917
War Diary	Trenches	03/04/1917	06/04/1917
War Diary	Billets Arras Front Trenches	08/04/1917	12/04/1917
War Diary	Support Line	13/04/1917	14/04/1917
War Diary	Trenches	06/04/1917	07/04/1917
War Diary	Arras Hutments Acq	15/04/1917	20/04/1917
War Diary	La Thieuloye	21/04/1917	30/04/1917
Miscellaneous		16/04/1917	16/04/1917
Miscellaneous	1st South African Infantry Regt	18/04/1917	18/04/1917
Operation(al) Order(s)	1st South African Infantry Regt. 19/4/17 Operation Order Of 19th April 1917	19/04/1917	19/04/1917
War Diary	La Thieuloye	01/05/1917	25/05/1917
War Diary	La Thieuloye	10/05/1917	31/05/1917
War Diary	Y. Huts	29/06/1917	29/06/1917
War Diary	Y. Huts. W Etrun	18/06/1917	28/06/1917
War Diary	Arras Y. Huts W Eturn	09/06/1917	17/06/1917
War Diary	Arras	01/06/1917	08/06/1917
War Diary	Y. Huts	01/07/1917	05/07/1917
War Diary	Simencourt	06/07/1917	27/07/1917
War Diary	Royoal Court	28/07/1917	28/07/1917
War Diary	Front Line Trescault	29/07/1917	31/07/1917
War Diary	Simen Court	12/07/1917	21/07/1917
War Diary	Front Line Trescault	01/08/1917	02/08/1917
Map	Trenches Corrected From Information Received Up To 21.8.17		
War Diary	Metz-En-Couture	03/08/1917	08/08/1917
War Diary	Trenches Trescault Section	09/08/1917	16/08/1917
War Diary	Ytres	17/08/1917	27/08/1917
War Diary	Achiet-le Petit	28/08/1917	11/09/1917
War Diary	Watou	12/09/1917	13/09/1917

War Diary	Brandhoek	14/09/1917	16/09/1917
War Diary	Ypres Frezenberg Sector	17/09/1917	22/09/1917
War Diary	Toronto Camp	23/09/1917	23/09/1917
War Diary	Winnizeele	24/09/1917	26/09/1917
War Diary	Arneke	27/09/1917	30/09/1917
Operation(al) Order(s)	1st Regt. South African Infantry. 25/9/17. South African Brigade. Report On Operations 20/21st Sept, 1917 S.W. Of Zonnebeke. Ref. Map. Frezenberg 1/10,000. Edn. 3.	25/09/1917	25/09/1917
Miscellaneous	1st Regt. South African Infantry, 25/9/17. South African Brigade	25/09/1917	25/09/1917
Operation(al) Order(s)	Messages despatched by 1st Regiment, South African Infantry, During Operations Of 20/22nd Sept. 1917.	20/09/1917	20/09/1917
Miscellaneous	1st South African Infantry Brigade.	25/09/1917	25/09/1917
War Diary	Arneke Area	01/10/1917	03/10/1917
War Diary	Moulle	04/10/1917	09/10/1917
War Diary	Brake Camp Reigersbg	10/10/1917	11/10/1917
War Diary	Canal Bank Ypres	12/10/1917	12/10/1917
War Diary	Ypres Cheddar Villa	13/10/1917	16/10/1917
War Diary	Front Line	17/10/1917	18/10/1917
War Diary	St. Pol-Sur Mer	28/10/1917	28/10/1917
War Diary	Oostdunkirk Bains	29/10/1917	31/10/1917
War Diary	Front Line Hubner	19/10/1917	19/10/1917
War Diary	Canal Bank	20/10/1917	22/10/1917
War Diary	Nouveau Monde	23/10/1917	23/10/1917
War Diary	Wormhout	24/10/1917	24/10/1917
War Diary	St Pol-Sur-Mer Nr Durkirk	25/10/1917	27/10/1917
War Diary	Oo. St Dunkirk Bains	01/11/1917	08/11/1917
War Diary	In Front Line Near Port Bams Section	09/11/1917	17/11/1917
War Diary	Yorkshire Camp La Panne	18/11/1917	25/11/1917
War Diary	Ergny	26/11/1917	04/12/1917
War Diary	Couzecourt	05/12/1917	12/12/1917
War Diary	Hutments	13/12/1917	14/12/1917
War Diary	Gouzecourt.	15/12/1917	28/12/1917
War Diary	Hutments Near Lins	29/12/1917	31/12/1917
War Diary	Gouzecourt	22/12/1917	25/12/1917
Heading	9th (Scottish) Division South African Infy Bde. 1st South African Infy Regt Jan-Feb 1918		
Heading	9th Div So. African Bde 1st Bn So. African Inf Reg Jan-Feb 1918		
War Diary	Bugade Reserve	25/01/1918	27/01/1918
War Diary	Left Sub Section Geozecourt Sector	28/01/1918	31/01/1918
War Diary	Don Camp Moislains	13/01/1918	24/01/1918
War Diary	Support Line Gouzecourt Sector	08/01/1918	08/01/1918
War Diary	Front Line Gouzecourt Sector	09/01/1918	12/01/1918
War Diary	Front Line Gouzecourt Sector	01/01/1918	04/01/1918
War Diary	Support Line Gouzecourt Sector	05/01/1918	07/01/1918
War Diary	G.H.Q Ros. Cappy	01/02/1918	28/02/1918

9TH SCOTTISH DIVISION
STH AFRICAN INFY. BDE.

1ST STH AFRICAN INFY REGT.
JUN – DEC 1916
DIARIES FOR APR & MAY 1916
ARE MISSING.

FROM DELTA WESTERN FORCE
~~EGYPT~~

1st South African Infantry
Regiment

Arrived Marseilles from Egypt
20th April 1916

Diaries for April, May &
June 1916 are missing

MAP.
Trench Map. 36.N.W.2. 1/10,000.   Copy No. 5.

                                                        13 MAY 1916

1st SOUTH AFRICAN INFANTRY BRIGADE

OPERATION ORDER No. 26.

1. **RELIEF.** The 10th and 11th H. L. I., will be relieved in reserve of Right Sector of Divisional Line by two Battalions of the 1st S. A. I. Brigade, on the 14th Inst.,

2. **ENTRAINING OF 10th and 11th H. L. I.,** On relief the H. L. I., Battalions will march to Steenwerck, and entrain for 15th Division area.

3. **MOVE OF 10th and 11th H. L. I.,** The 10th H. L. I., will commence to move at 9 am. and the 11th H. L. I., at 11 a.m. Parties to move at strength not exceeding a platoon, 300 yards distance between parties.

    Use will be made, as far as possible, of the following three roads:-

    (1) Leading S.W., from Chapelle Rompue.

    (2) Leading W. from point C.13.d.1½.7½.

    (3) Leading S. from same point.

4. **TRENCH MAPS, etc.,** All trench maps, log books, aeroplane and panorama photographs will be handed over.

5. **REPORTING COMPLETION OF MOVE.** The Officers Commanding 10th and 11th H. L. I., respectively will report by wire to Brigade Headquarters when their last parties have moved from Le Bizet.

6. **TRANSPORT.** Three motor lorries will be provided for each of the 10th and 11th H. L. I., - Reporting at 9 a.m. on the 14th inst.,

    The first line Transport of the 10th H. L. I., will be handed in to 9th Divisional Train, La Creche, not later than 3 p.m. on the 14th inst.,

    The first line Transport of the 11th H. L. I., will march by road to Bethune, 1 aving at 8 a.m. on the 14th inst., On arrival at Bethune it will park in the Marche aux Chevaux, where a guide from the 15th Division will meet it.

7. **TRANSPORT LINES.** The Officer Commanding the 1st S. A. I., will detail an Officer to take over the Transport Lines of the 10th H. L. I., at 6.30 a.m. on the 14th inst., Map Reference, B.17.Central.

    The Officer Commanding the 4th S. A. I., will detail and Officer to take over the Transport Lines of the 11th H. L. I., at 6.30 a.m. on the 14th inst., Map Reference, B.3.d.6.6.

    In each case the Officer will take over from the 10th and 11th H. L. I., respectively the Reserve Ammunition which is kept at the Transport Lines.

8. **STORES.** All stores will be handed over on the 13th inst.,

Operation Order No.28.

(2)

9. **LEWIS GUNS.** The 10th and 11th H. L. I., will each hand over one Lewis Gun to the 4th S. A. I., on the 13th inst., Transport for same will be provided from 10th H. L. I.,

10. **BILLETTING PARTIES.** The Officers Commanding 2nd and 3rd S.A.I., will detail Billetting Parties of one Officer and 6 other ranks to take over billets from 10th and 11th H. L. I., at 7 a.m. on the 14th inst.,

11. **MOVE OF PORTIONS OF 2nd and 3rd S. A. I.** Those portions of the 2nd and 3rd S. A. I., in Armentieres on the morning of the 14th inst., will move into Le Bizet billets, S. and N. Rest Battalions respectively, on that evening. Parties to move at strength not exceeding a platoon. 300 yds between parties.

    Leading platoon to move off at 7.45 p.m.

    Report to be sent to Brigade Headquarters when all men are in billets.

12. **SIGNAL OFFICES, LE BIZET.** The Officers Commanding the 2nd and 3rd S. A. I., will arrange to take over the Signal Offices of the Rest Battalions, S. and N. Le Bizet, respectively, at 9 a.m. on the 14th inst.,

13. **COMMAND.** The Command of the Battalions in the Line will pass to the Officers Commanding the 1st and 4th S. A. I., on the 14th May at 4 p.m. — the Officer Commanding the 1st S. A. I., taking the Right Sub-sector, and the Officer Commanding the 4th S. A. I., the Left Sub-sector.

Acknowledge.

Mitchell Bates
Major
Bde. Major
1st SAI Bde

Copy No.1 to 10th H. L. I.,	Copy No.9 to 27th Inf. Brigade.
2 11th H. L. I.;	10 O.C. Bde M.G. Coy.
3 1st S. A. I.;	11 O.C. L. T. M. Bty.
4 2nd do	12 O.C. 107th Co. A.S.C.
5 3rd do	13 O.C. 2nd Arty Group.
6 4th do	14 O. i/c Bde Sig Section.
7 9th Division.	15 Office Copy.
8 26th Inf. Brigade.	

Issued by Orderly at................

WAR DIARY
or
INTELLIGENCE SUMMARY.

Army Form C. 2118.

July

Vol III

Vol 4 July

Place	Date	Hour	Summary of Events and Information	Remarks and references to Appendices
	1.6.16	6.30pm	The Regiment marched to Bailleul and halted at MOULENACHER STANDING CAMP in the MORBECQUE AREA.	
	2.6.16	2 pm	Marched to WITTERNESS.	
	3.6.16		Marched to ERNY ST JULIEN, where the Regiment was to undergo training.	
	4.6.16		Was spent in Washing & Bathing	
	5.6.16		The following training was carried out by Companies.	
	6.6.16		1 hour Coy orders & Arms Drill	
			1 " Bayonet fighting	
			2 " Swing	
			1 " Bombing	
			2 " Attack practice	
			½ " Musketry	
	7.6.16		A draft of 50 men joined the Regiment on this date. Training was carried out as on the previous day.	
	8.		do.	
	9.		The Battalion carried out an attack scheme from 9am-12 noon.	8

Date	Hour	Summary of Events and Information	Remarks reference Append
		in the formation laid down in 9th Divisional instructions in the "Organization of a Battalion for the Attack". Each Coy carried out 1½ hours training in Bombing Bayonet fighting in Bayonet fighting in the afternoon.	
10.6.16	7.30 AM	The Battalion paraded at 7.30 am to practise "Artillery Formations". In the afternoon Coys carried out the same training as on the previous day.	
11.6.16		The Brigade carried out an attack on a frontage of 900 yards. The formation adopted was as laid down in Divisional training instructions; that is the frontage was divided into two, and a section of 450 yards allotted to a Battalion. The 2nd and 4th Battalions were in advance supported by 3rd and 1st Battalion respectively.	
12.6.16		6 hours training was carried out by each Company, particular attention being paid to marching, advancing in line of sections or to a given objective	

WAR DIARY
or
INTELLIGENCE SUMMARY.
(Erase heading not required.)

Place	Date	Hour	Summary of Events and Information	Remarks and references to Appendices
	13.6.16		Training was carried out by Coys in the morning. Men were granted leave to attend the Brigade Horse Show in the afternoon.	
	14.6.16		Training was carried out under Coy arrangements. Received Orders to entrain at BERGUETTE at 11.40 AM on 15.6.16.	
	15.6.16		Marched out of ERNY ST JULIEN at 5.30 AM arrived at BERGUETTE at 9.30 AM. Trained left at 11.40 AM. Detrained at LONGEAU at 8 p.m. Marched to LONGPRE arriving there at 11.30 p.m.	
	16.6.16		Training was carried out under Coy arrangements	
	17.6.16	9 am	The Battalion paraded for a Route March	
	18.6.16		Sunday Church Parades were held as follows:- C of E 9 am. 5 Officers & 178 other Ranks of B Coy went to Corbie on Wesleyans 12 noon duty. R.C. 10.30 am	
			less B Coy	
	19.6.16	9 pm	Battalion paraded for a Route March	
	20.6.16		Battalion less B Coy carried out an attack practice	
	21.6.16		Training was carried out under Coy arrangements from 10.30 am–12.30 pm. The Battalion – less 300 men & B Officers detailed for duty, and B Coy in trench area – attended

Army Form C. 2118.

WAR DIARY
or
INTELLIGENCE SUMMARY.
(Erase heading not required.)

Instructions regarding War Diaries and Intelligence Summaries are contained in F. S. Regs., Part II. and the Staff Manual respectively. Title pages will be prepared in manuscript.

89

Place	Date	Hour	Summary of Events and Information	Remarks and references to Appendices
	22.6.16	9 AM	a "Gas Demonstration" at training ground N.E. of SAN SAUVEUR. The Battalion -less B Coy. marched to the training ground N.E. of SAN SAUVEUR. Leaving by Coys. was carried out from 10.15 AM - 12.30 PM and from 2 - 3.30 PM the Battalion practised "the Attack" over the trenches.	
	23.6.16	1.30 PM	The Battalion -less B Coy.- marched out of LONGPRE to entrain at AILLY for CORBIE. Arrived at CORBIE at 8 PM and marched out to VAUX ROAD camp.	
	24.6.16	2.30 PM	Marched to WELLCOME WOOD	
	25.6.16		Coy arrangements.	
	26.6.16		do Drawing equipment, etc.	
	27.6.16	9.30 PM	March to BOIS LES CELESTINES	
	28.6.16		Remained BOIS LES CELESTINES In training army to work.	
	29.6.16		Two hours training and Route March 6.30 PM - 8.30 PM.	
	30.6.16		Two hours training. Marched to GROVETOWN VALLEY 9.30 PM arriving 11.30 PM. Transport arrived 4. AM. 1.7.16	
	1.7.16		Remained GROVETOWN awaiting orders. 5th Brigade were being held in Reserve.	

1st S.A. Inf. Regt WAR DIARY

JULY 1916 INTELLIGENCE SUMMARY

Vol 4

Place	Date	Hour	Summary of Events and Information	Remarks and references to Appendices
	1.7.16		Remained GROVE TOWN awaiting orders for S.A. Bde as being held in reserve.	
TRIGGER WOOD	3.7.16		The Regt march to TRIGGER WOOD.	
	3.7.16		Remained at TRIGGER WOOD	
GERMAN 1st System	4.7.16	8.45 pm	The Regt moved forward to old GERMAN 1st system. Trenches and occupied same as follows A Coy, NORD ALLEY. B Coy TRAIN ALLEY. C Coy GLATZ REDOUBT. D Coy CHIMNEY TRENCH and BRIQUETERIE	
MONTAUBAN MARICOURT	5.7.16		Casualties for 5.7.16: 4 O.R. wounded	
	6.7.16		" 2 O.R. killed 5 O.R. wounded	
	7.7.16		" 2 O.R. killed 10 O.R. wounded — Regt relieved	
			by 18th Manchester Regt at about 11 pm and returned to Billets in 1st line Trenches MARICOURT. Reliever have - been. carried - out in accordance to Am 3/7/16	
Billets du 8.7.16			Casualties 9 O.R. wounded	
1st Line Trench	9.7.16		" 10 O.R. "	
MARICOURT	10.7.16		" 2 O.R. killed 7 wounded	
	11.7.16		" 6 O.R. wounded	
	12.7.16			

Dawson

WAR DIARY or INTELLIGENCE SUMMARY

Army Form C. 2118.

Place	Date	Hour	Summary of Events and Information	Remarks and references to Appendices
Sand	13/7/16		6 O.R. wounded. Shell fire. Received orders that Bn would attack the following morning. The S.O.B. being in reserve & that the Bty would be called on first. The line Bazentin le Gd - Bazentin le Petit - Neuville 3 A.M. Regt. ready to move by 2 A.M. Shortly afterwards other information was sent for to Bde H.Q. & instructed to take this up to Montauban Alley - a C.T. running NE from a point about 100 x from the N.W. corner of Montauban. This was complied with about 11 A.M.	
	14/7/16		Col Dawson was called to H.Q. of 27th Bde & informed by the Brigadier that the 26 & 27 Bdes were holding the Southern portion of LONGUEVAL but were held up by M.G. sunken in the Northern portion of the village. Col Dawson received verbal instructions to reply this regt in a wood known along the line held by the 26/27 - 15 x x x to attack the remainder of the village at 2 P.M. There would be a preliminary bombardment lasting for 15 minutes, the last 5' of which it would be intense. The objective of the attack was to be the line marked on a skeleton plan in pencil. The demonstration	

WAR DIARY OR INTELLIGENCE SUMMARY

Army Form C. 2118.

Place	Date	Hour	Summary of Events and Information	Remarks and references to Appendices
	14.7.16		advance to LONGUEVAL to ascertain the situation, giving orders to Major Bryson to hurry up the regt in 2 lines of sections in file. There was some artillery & machine gun fire though little field or heavy artillery fire. The coy advanced towards the objective & to Coy on the right supported by C & B on the left supported by D. It was known on the left supported by G.D. It was known accurately difficult to recognise the objective & not having been definitely the ground which in addition was much altered by the shelling put first & hope Had Officers who had received a very elementary training in map reading would be able to [illegible] his position. This coy was willing pushed on though the wood to the East of the village was shelled. I took up my H.Q at the point marked C. At about 4 pm I received a report from the O.C. to Coy that he had reached what he thought was his objective & taken a report came in from the O.C. A Co to the effect that he had occupied a certain trench, the position of which was not clear from the report. Both officers added that they could advance no further owing to heavy M.G. fire on the North & North East. Stcenwhich was that A & B Co occupied the trench marked D & A Co. that marked E.E. which was	92

WAR DIARY / INTELLIGENCE SUMMARY

Army Form C. 2118.

Place	Date	Hour	Summary of Events and Information	Remarks and references to Appendices
LONGUEVAL	14.7.16		It appears C Co. was then in the trenches marked G & C about the centre of the line. About 6 p.m. the O.C., C Co. endeavoured to surround & capture a M.G. which was firing from a trench called the chalkpit marked H. In trying to do this the M.O., C Co. — Capt. JENKINS, was wounded, also Lieut. LARMUTH of D Co. The casualties in the coming of the afternoon were 4 officers & about 50 other ranks, the other two officers being Lt. DENT & Lt. REID being the other two. C Co. was withdrawn to the trenches marked G.	C Co. withdrew to the line D.
		11 p.m.	Received most urgent orders from G.O.C. 27th 13th that the M.G. holding up the advance must be captured tonight & all parties ordered to send up fresh schemes to carry this out. Three parties under Lt. HENRY, BATES & BURGESS, were detailed & started at about 12 midnight. That under Lt. BURGESS returned soon & reported that the M.G. at A was no longer there & the trench was clear. The other two parties returned after daylight reporting that they had searched the houses on both sides of NORTH street until they suddenly came under a very heavy M.G. fire from a house marked J, Verey lights being thrown at them & Very lights sent up. They had no casualties however.	
	15.7.16			

93

WAR DIARY or INTELLIGENCE SUMMARY

Army Form C. 2118.

Place	Date	Hour	Summary of Events and Information	Remarks and references to Appendices
LONGUEVAL	15/7/16		They established themselves in a house opposite J & endeavoured to cause the M. Gunner to withdraw. Arrangements were now made by the C.O. to set up a trench mortar & Stokes gun. The one done is in the afternoon, the fire from the T.M. destroyed & set fire to the house from which the M.G. was firing. Altogether 7 houses were destroyed, 4 of which were found. One of the enemy was blown up into the sky. C.T.D. coys: must be [crossed out] by flying splinters (?). Two attempts of the portion of the town order were received from the B.C. Major 6.a. 7.5.a.m.? that the portion of the town in possession of the enemy was to be attacked at 10 a.m. The Royals to attack from the West & H 2 companies of the 1st S.A.S. from the South. The would be a preparation by T.M. & Stokes guns. The necessary arrangements were made & orders were issued that at 10 a.m. A bombing action should rush across from the trench marked Q into the German trench about 40 x to the North & bomb along it. A. Coy advancing to the North from the trench E & 1 Platoon of B. from the trench D, the objective being the Northern boundary of the wood. [Two companies of the 1st S.A.S. would support the attack]. At 10 a.m. a start was made by all of these except the platoon of B. to which was delayed by a platoon of B. to which lodged into the trench by mistake. The parties advancing were immediately under an	BELLVILLE J.H. wood
	16/7/16			

94

WAR DIARY or INTELLIGENCE SUMMARY

Place	Date	Hour	Summary of Events and Information	Remarks and references to Appendices
LONGUEVAL	16/7/16		exceedingly heavy M.G. fire from nothing less than 3 M.Gs. were practically annihilated. No further progress was possible & although the T.M. & Stokes guns fired on the enemy's position at intervals throughout the day, the M.Gs were not silenced. The 2 companies of the 6. S.A.S. had been ordered to remain in support along PRINCE'S STREET but for an unknown reason did not do so. Some parties of them occupied the trench marked E.E. St had also been arranged that the Co.7 of the 1st S.A.I. which was holding the line of the STRAND, on their orders to C.O. 2nd S.A.I. should advance to the WEST, should they also were held up by M.G. fire. At sunset no progress had been made, nor was there any hope of making any. In the course of the day the 90 Co 17 Bde - S.A. Bde moved up the trench D. I came to the conclusion that the hostile position, were hastily organised strong point, which could only be taken after heavy artillery preparation. In the course of the operations 2/Lt ENGLISH displayed great courage & coolness in trench D. in leading the enemy firing on them over the parapet whenever they moved along the trench, that it was possible for the snipers to pick their shots above the parapet without being fired at individually	

Place	Date	Hour	Summary of Events and Information	Remarks and references to Appendices
	16/7/16		The enemy suffered a fair number of casualties for both Their machine gun along the trench from our place together, Lt ENGLISH & his men fired hard at them with LEWIS guns & rifles. The following men displayed great bravery. Lt OWEN No 4073 Pte W.F. FAULDS No 893 A/Cpl G.F. BAKER & No 4787 Pte A. ESTMENT under the following circumstances. Lt OWEN attempted to run across to the German trench at 10 p.m. with the bombing section between ball wounded & lay in the open about half way i.e. 20 yards short of the trench. Lt Col m. the German The 3 men in question in broad daylight went over the parapet under an exceedingly heavy M.G. & rifle fire & picked up Lt OWEN & carried him back. Pte BAKER being severely wounded in doing so. The casualties during the day were :- killed Capt MILLER, G.S. & Lt PARSONS, C.D. 2nd Lt HAHN E.A.L. 2/Lt BROWN, A.E. 2nd Lt HAARHOFF A.C. wounded 2/Lt CRAIG, R.K. Capt & Adjt TO PRIDAY. 2nd Lt CHAPMAN, H.G. 2/Lt TEMPANY, W. Missing 2nd Lt HOLLINGWORTH, J.M. It was impossible to ascertain the casualties of other ranks owing to the heavy being left out & it being impossible to get in the severely wounded until after dark – also owing to parties of the men still being unable to rejoin for some days. members of them of being exact.

War Diary

16.7.16 — At 10 p.m. the C.O. returned to Batt. H.Q. bringing orders that the 2 Coys of 6th SAS were to occupy the trenches prepared opposite D Coy.

17.7.16 — At 9 A.M. our heavy artillery opened fire on the German trenches & strong point & trench opposite & 40 yds distant from that occupied by Lt. ENGLISH. The latter had had no previous warning of the bombardment, but removed his men without casualties. At about 12 noon Lt. English & his men were withdrawn to the trenches previously occupied by D Co., the KOSB's taking over the trench of D.

18.7.16 — Hostile shelling on DELVILLE WOOD & LONGUEVAL very heavy. At about 8 A.M. orders were received to send 50 men to reinforce C & D Coys of 1st SAI in the STRAND. This was carried out. Shortly after noon 3 men of the party returned & said they had orders to retire, there being only about 12 men left of the original 50. This report was forwarded to Bde. H.Q. also others to the effect that the two companies of this regt. had suffered very severely - principally from shell fire, & had given ground. At 3.30 P.M. Lt. Col. Dawson received orders to take up all the men of the 1st & 4th SAS that were available to the STRAND & North East Boundary of the wood to reinforce the 2 coys under Major BURGES. These orders were followed at a very short interval by others, brought by Lt. ROSEBY that on arrival at DELVILLE WOOD officers patrols were to be sent out to ascertain the situation. The numbers available were about 80 men

18.7.16 of A & B Coys 1st S.A.I. & a similar number of the 4th S.A.I. The hostile barrage was at that time exceedingly heavy & it seemed very doubtful if it could be traversed without heavy loss. At 4.10 p.m. the party set out. Officers had in the meantime come in from the Northern & North Eastern boundaries of the wood, who reported that the troops had been practically annihilated by the artillery fire & there were none left to hold the wood.

The members of the 1st & 4th S.A.I.s were put by Col Dawson in the old German front line trenches, S.W. of the village, while it was ascertained where our front troops were. Men of all units were at this time streaming out of the village, disorganised & without officers & it was reported that the enemy had occupied the village. As however it was ascertained that the 3rd S.A.I. were still holding their support trenches in BUCHANAN ST. Col Dawson took the men into the town & put them into the trenches at K Stores which were held very lightly or not at all, those on the left being strongly held by the 26th Bde. Germans were at this time seen in the wood about 200ᵡ ENE of the church. At about 9 p.m. a report was received from Major Hunt comdg the remnant of the 4th S.A.I. that he was in touch with the 3rd S.A.I. About the same time Sgt VINCENT 1st S.A.I. brought a message from the O.C. 3rd S.A.I. to the effect that his left was in the air & reinforcements were urgently needed to connect with the next unit on the left.

Bombs & S.A.A. were urgently needed also 99

18/7/16 Immediately on receipt of this, Col Dawson
despatched the L.T.M. detachment & some details
under Lt PHILLIPS, over 100 in number, to the
O.C. 3rd S.A.I. Some 25 men of 4th S.A.I. were sent
shortly afterwards. At about 11 P.M. Col Dawson
went to the A.Q. of 3rd S.A.I. & found it full of wounded
officers, there being no 3rd S.A.I. stretcher bearers
left. It not being possible
to obtain other stretcher bearers, some 16 men of 1st S.A.I.
were told off for this duty. These were taken round
by Capt W E STYLE who was wounded in the throat while
taking the wounded out. This officer had taken
over the duties of Adjt when Capt PRIDAY was wounded.
While this was going on a message arrived from Bde H.Q.
to the effect that all regts of the S.A. Bde were to be
relieved by the 26th Bde & that the S.A. Bde was to return
to the Talus Boise.

19/7/16 No regt coming to relieve the S.A. Regts.
The D.L.I. having arrived in the town, Col Dawson went
to see Col GORDON of the Gordons who was responsible
for the disposal of troops & suggested that this regt should
relieve the 3rd S.A.I. in the wood. Col Gordon agreed &
went with Col Dawson to the C.O. of the D.L.I. giving
him orders in the presence of Col Dawson to take
his regt to relieve the 3rd S.A.I. The leading company
marched off for this purpose with Lt PHILLIPS as
guide. The trench where the 1st & 4th S.A.I. were, being
now very congested Col Dawson asked Col Gordon if he
might withdraw his men. Col Gordon acquiescing, the

19.7.16   Necessary orders were given & the men filed out as day was breaking.

The total number of 1st S.A.I. who marched back from LONGUEVAL from Batt. H.Q. was 6 officers & 160 other ranks.

Some members of C & D Coys came in at various times, & others joined the 3rd S.A.I. in their trenches. From these it appears that with the exception of the few who returned, the two companies were practically annihilated.

The first casualty list made out shewed

	killed	wounded	missing
Officers	7	14	3
Other ranks	87	352	165

during the period 14th to 19th July. Of the missing many were undoubtedly either killed, or wounded & evacuated through other clearing stations.

Among the killed was Major E.T. BURGES, an officer of the 5th South African Mounted Rifles. He was a most capable officer who had done invaluable work as adjutant during the trying period in which the regiment was trained & disciplined, also throughout the Egyptian campaign. Undoubtedly the high standard of efficiency attained by the regt. was due to the untiring efforts of Major Burges. He was a most gallant officer & his loss is a heavy blow to the regt.

The behaviour of the regt. through a most trying time was beyond all praise. They were 5 nights without rest & suffered exceedingly heavy casualties, principally from

19.7.16 shell & M.G. fire, but [illegible]
[illegible lines]
they were never in the slightest degree demoralised
or shaken & when returning to LONGUEVAL on
the afternoon of the 18th under an artillery fire which
appeared impassable, their one desire was to get to
close quarters with the enemy. It would be impossible
to find better troops.

20th Marched from Talus Boisé to HAPPY VALLEY
where there was a draft of 79 men awaiting the
regt. All transport & details rejoined.
A further draft of 6 men reported later
in the day.

21st The draft which had been
awaiting the regiment paraded from
9 a.m. - 12 noon. They were exercised
in platoon and arms drill.
Another draft of 95 men reported during
the course of the morning.
List of casualties which occurred during
operations from 1st - 21st July as far
as could be ascertained

Officers Killed   7
  "   Wounded   13
  "   Missing & Wounded 1
  "   Missing   3
Other Ranks Killed   100
  "   Wounded 403
  "   Missing   98

22nd July — The draft paraded for instruction in coming operations drill under Sgt Myt from 9 am – 11 am.
At 12 noon Brig. Gen. Lukin CB CMG DSO addressed the Brigade and thanked them for excellent behaviour during the operations from 4th – 19th July.
At 2 pm the Battalion less C & D paraded for purpose of finding billets at BRAY
At 3 pm C & D Coys proceeded to billets at BRAY

Casualties :- None of the missing being reported for duty having remained with Lt. Col. THACKERAY of 3rd Regt. in DEL- VILLE WOOD
Number of missing to date — 89

23rd July — Battalion marched out from HAPPY VALLEY to MERINCOURT where they entrained. Arrived at HANGEST at 8.30 pm Marched to LONG and arrived at about 10.15 pm. Battalion was billeted here.

24th July — Bathing parade & kit inspection under company arrangements.

25th July — Bathing parade under company arrangements. Battalion marched to LONGPRE at 11.15 pm where it entrained.

26th July — Arrived Bryas 6.30 am. Marched to Magnicourt.

27th July — Left MAGNICOURT at 1.15 pm by road.
Arrived FREVILLERS at 2.15 pm.
Lt. Col. F.S. DAWSON assumed command of Bde.
during temporary absence of Brig-Gen.
H.T. LUKIN C.B. C.M.G. D.S.O.
Feet and Rifle Inspection.

28th July — Company Training including
Bombing, Trench Warfare, Gas Helmet Drill
Bayonet Fighting.

29th July — Brig. Gen. Lukin re-assumes command
of the Bde.
Training as for 28th inst.

30th July — No change - Training as for 28th inst.

31st July — No change - Training as for 28th inst.

F.S. Dawson Lt Col
O.C. 1 - S.A. Inf
1-8-16

104

Army Form C. 2118.

WAR DIARY
or
INTELLIGENCE SUMMARY.
(Erase heading not required.)

1st K.A. Infantry

Instructions regarding War Diaries and Intelligence Summaries are contained in F. S. Regs., Part II. and the Staff Manual respectively. Title pages will be prepared in manuscript.

Place	Date	Hour	Summary of Events and Information	Remarks and references to Appendices
FREVILLERS	1.8.16	6.30pm	No change — Training as for 28th July.	
"	2.8.16	6.30pm	No change — Training as for 28th July.	
"	3.8.16	8.30pm	Coys. proceeded to Baths at FRESSICOURT. New Clothing issued. 21 N.C.O & men reported from Hospital — 6 from Base ROUEN.	
"	4.8.16	6.30pm	Training as for 28th July. 2 Officers — 80 other ranks reported from Base Depot. ROUEN.	O.R. O.R. 610 197 Brockman 516.
"	5.8.16	6.30pm	Brigade inspected by Army Commander at 3pm. Army Commander welcomed Brigade to 4th Army and expressed himself as being very pleased with general turnout. 18 N.C.O & men reported from Hospital — 1 N.C.O from Base ROUEN.	On Parade Officers Noon Ranks
"	6.8.16	8.30am	Church Parade.	
"	7.8.16	8am	No change — Training as for 28th July.	
"	8.8.16	6.30am	No change — Training as for 28th July. Inspection of Boots, Gas Helmets, Iron Rations etc. C.O. inspected all Billets	
"	9.8.16	8.10pm	Physical Training, Bayonet fighting etc. C.O. inspected all Billets	
"	10.8.16	8.20pm	His Majesty the KING visited FREVILLERS arriving by M.T. at 7.30 & 9.30 & 10.30.	

WAR DIARY
or
INTELLIGENCE SUMMARY.
(Erase heading not required.)

Army Form C. 2118.

Place	Date	Hour	Summary of Events and Information	Remarks and references to Appendices
VILLERS AU BOIS	18.8.16	8.30 a.m.	Training – Forenoon – Coy. Arrangements – 3 p.m. Route March – Cancelled owing to heavy rain.	
"	19.8.16	8.30 a.m.	Training – Forenoon – Coy. Arrangements – 3 p.m. Route March – Cancelled owing to heavy rain. E.O. 1 offr & 4 N.C.O's per Coy. visited Trench Area.	
VILLERS AU BOIS	20.8.16	6.30 p.m.	Divine Service. Two Coys. on Working party for 5th Divn. R.E's.	
		8 John 4 a.m.		
	21.8.16	8.30 a.m.	Training. A & B Coys. 9 a.m. to 11.30 a.m. C & D Coys. Working Party.	
		2 a/w 20 E		
	22.8.16	4 John	Training. C & D Coys. 9 a.m. to 11 a.m. A & B Coys. Working Party.	
Support Line BERTHONVAL	23.8.16	3.20 p.m.	Left VILLERS AU BOIS. Arrived at 12.45 p.m. by Battn. Arrived BERTHONVAL 3.30 p.m. Took over from 1st Bat'n E.L. lines in for which attached.	
	24.8.16	3 p.m.	Working and carrying parties, filling 100 offr N.C.O. men relieved for working parties. R.E. supervision. Remainder of B's employed in cleaning trenches, improving old trenches & making new dug-outs etc. in R.A. Area.	

106

WAR DIARY
INTELLIGENCE SUMMARY
(Erase heading not required.)

Army Form C. 2118.

Place	Date	Hour	Summary of Events and Information	Remarks and references to Appendices
FREVILLERS	10.8.16	8.20pm	at 11.20 am. His Majesty's visit was quite informal. The regiment lined either side of the street in fatigue dress and followed His Majesty to the end of the village, heartily cheering & followed His Majesty's car on his leaving. During His Majesty's walk through the village he conversed to several ranks viz No.913 Pte. W.A.Els. a typical S.A. Colonist who has seen much service. 8pm - The regiment carried out night operation returning to Billets @ 11.15pm.	
"	"	"		
FREVILLERS	11.8.16	8.30pm	Training 4 hours. Bombing, Trench Warfare, Bayonet Fighting etc.	
"	12.8.16	8.30pm	Church Service.	
"	13.8.16	8.30pm	Training as for 11th inst. during forenoon. 8pm. Night Operations.	
"	14.8.16	8.30pm	Training as for 11th inst.	
VILLERS AU BOIS	15.8.16	8.30pm	Moved by road from FREVILLERS by at 3pm. arrived VILLERS AU BOIS at 6pm.	
"	16.8.16	8.30pm	Regiment bathed. Parades under Coy. Arrangements.	
"	17.8.16	8.30pm	Training 2 hours - Bombing, Bayonet Fighting etc. Route march 3pm.	

108

MAGNETIC

ERSATZ ALLEY.

ALHAMBRA.

B. M.G.

B.

St. MARTINS LANE.

B.H.Q.
C.H.Q.
PIONEER DUMP
C.H.Q.
A.P.

RAILWAY

SAA
B.
O.P.
DUMP
G.
M.G.
V.S.

S.A.A.
B. M.G.
L.G.

ARRAS ALLEY

ARRAS ROAD

D

C.H.Q.

M.G.

To LIVERPOOL DUMP

COLISEUM.

DEAD END ALLEY

WORTLEY AV.

DUCKWALK.

Co.Res SAA
B. B.   M.G.

V.S.
G.
B.

C.H.Q.

G.
B.   CENTRAL AV.

V.S.
G.
C.H.Q.
O.P.

CENTRAL AV.

REFERENCE.

B.H.Q. — Battln. Head Qrs
C.H.Q. — Company "
A.P. — Aid Post
B.D. — Battln. Dump
D — Company
S.A.A. — S.A.A. Store
B. — Bomb Store
G. — Gas Gong
V.S. — Vermorel Sprayer
M.G. — Brigade Mach. Gun
L.G. — Lewis Gun
O.P. — Observation Post

Place	Date	Hour	Summary of Events and Information	Remarks and references to Appendices
BERTHONVAL	31.5.16	9.30pm	and returned at daybreak. Enemy wire broken in parts. No hostile parties encountered. Working parties on for 30th inst. Commander of regt. refraining damage to trenches caused by bad weather.	

Lawson Lt. Col.
Commdg. 1st S.A.I.

WAR DIARY
or
INTELLIGENCE SUMMARY.
(Erase heading not required.)

Army Form C. 2118.

Place	Date	Hour	Summary of Events and Information	Remarks and references to Appendices
Support Line				
BERTHONVAL	25.8.16	8.30pm	No change.	
"	26.8.16	8.30pm	No change.	
"	27.8.16	8.30pm	No change.	
"	28.8.16	8.30pm	No change.	
"	29.8.16	8.30pm	No change.	
"	30.8.16	8.30pm	The regiment relieved the 3rd S.A.I. in Front line BERTHONVAL II commencing at 7am. Relief completed by 10.30 am. Look over working parties from 3rd Regt. totaling 98 O/prs NCOs & men. The following honours & awards were granted to Offrs & Other Ranks for work performed in DELVILLE WOOD, vide Div. Routine Order of 22.8.16 & Div. Routine Order of 29.8.16 - Military Cross - 2/Lt. F.H. ENGLISH. D.C.M. - 706 Pte(R/Cpl) HEALY V.M. M.M. - 4172 Pte LOUBSER A.I. - MILITARY MEDAL. X244 R/Cpl. TAYLOR J. 893 Pte BAKER G. 4757 L/Cpl EJSMENT. A. 4798 Pte BAKER T.T. 4278 L/Cpl. HORT G.A. 906 Pte HOLLIDAY T.H. 5627 Pte (L/Cpl) HARRIS W.F. Weather bad - Rain and very wet.	
"	31.8.16	8.30pm	Three patrols under Lts. Forbes, Stapleton & Macdonell went out at 1am	Out.

Army Form C. 2118.

Vol 6

1/8 R. Regt

WAR DIARY
or
INTELLIGENCE SUMMARY.
(Erase heading not required.)

Instructions regarding War Diaries and Intelligence Summaries are contained in F. S. Regs., Part II. and the Staff Manual respectively. Title pages will be prepared in manuscript.

Place	Date	Hour	Summary of Events and Information	Remarks and references to Appendices
Support line	1-9-16	8:30pm	1699 Pte WALLACE, W.T. wounded, severe, back, shrapnel. Gas alert on.	
BERTHONVAL			Two officers + N.C.O's patrols went out at about 11pm. No sign of enemy. No man's land.	
"	2-9-16	8:30pm	Enemy appear to be more active. 1 Officer + 1 N.C.O patrol went out. No casualties	
"	3-9-16	8:30pm	Regiment was relieved by 5/Cameron Highlanders + 1 Coy/ A + S Hrs. Retired to billets at MAISNIL BOUCHE. Weather bad. Last Coy arrived billets 11pm	
MAISNIL BOUCHE.	4-9-16	8:30pm	Weather stormy. No change.	
"	5-9-16	8:30pm	D: Presentation of Medal Ribbons by Rt Hon The Earl of Derby at CAMBLAIN L'ABBE. 250 men sent to the parade. Remainder of regiment carried out training	
Front line	6-9-16	8:30pm	Relieved 1/1 R Scots + 1 Batt 1/K.O.S.B in Front line, Left Sector, CARENCY. Relief completed by 2:30 am. No 4415 Pte HURLEY, W.A. killed - shell fire. Trenches in bad condition. Gas alert on.	
CARENCY II				
"	7-9-16	8:30pm	No patrols out. 5034 Pte BOTHA, F wounded, slight, shrapnel. 8047 Pte ALLEN, T. shell shock. Gas alert on.	

WAR DIARY / INTELLIGENCE SUMMARY

Army Form C. 2118.

Place	Date	Hour	Summary of Events and Information	Remarks and references to Appendices
Front Line CUINCHY to BRICKSTACKS	28.9.16	8.30p	Enemy Artillery very active with light batteries. Casualties:— 1910 Pte WALE R.S., 1238 Rfn. WHITE B. (Killed) 1162 Pte TAYLOR R.H. 1556 Pte TAYLOR R.H. wounded.	
"	29.9.16	8.30p	Enemy aeroplanes more aggressive and no general behaviour points to his being soon relieved within part of hours. Between 9.30 and 9.50 p.m. sniping was plainly heard coming from German support lines, and from the direction of GIVENCHY — it sounded as if nine shells were being dispersed. Heavy trench mortar fired nine shells into our lines damaging our trenches. Two patrols were sent out. No enemy seen. Casualties:— No. 9538 Pte. BADGER E.E., 7138 Pte BADGER G. (Killed), Pte. J.Gp. FINCHAM G, wounded.	
"	30.9.16	8.30p	The whole section has been shelled at intervals with "Whizbangs". Little damage was done. A large number of rifle grenades were sent over during the day, the majority being "duds". Three of them were killed in our saps by enemy snipers during the early hours of this morning. Three shells were sent into our lines by "MINENWERFER" doing slight damage. Our artillery active. Casualties:—	112

Army Form C. 2118.

WAR DIARY
or
INTELLIGENCE SUMMARY
(Erase heading not required.)

Instructions regarding War Diaries and Intelligence Summaries are contained in F. S. Regs., Part II. and the Staff Manual respectively. Title pages will be prepared in manuscript.

Place	Date	Hour	Summary of Events and Information	Remarks and references to Appendices
Front line CARENCY II	11.9.16	8.30 pm	At 10.30 pm Rockets were sent up by enemy in pairs, each of these burst into two red lights (like lakes tongues) these were immediately followed by considerable shell fire lasting 20 minutes. This was in retaliation to the counter sent off by the mining by R.E. MINENWERFER shells were again fired into our line doing no damage. Our artillery active. Two Germans wearing White's have been seen. An enemy seen in the sector in the past was cup. Casualties 1 killed and 2 wounded.	
"	12.9.16	8.30 pm	Enemy has been very quiet. An Officers patrol went out to examine the wire. No enemy seen. Our artillery very active. Casualties 2 killed one wounded.	
"	13.9.16	8.30 pm	Enemy very quiet and does not attempt to retaliate. A successful raid was carried out by battalion on our right, during which two su (tunnels) 4-4.19pm enemy sent over very hot artillery fire.	
"	14.9.16	8.30 pm	Enemy quiet. Our artillery active. Casualties 1 killed 2 wounded	
"	15.9.16	8.30 pm	Enemy retaliates more vigorously than usual. At 10.5 pm enemy artillery opened vigorous bombardment of whole sector in reply to Stokes	

13

Army Form C. 2118.

WAR DIARY
or
INTELLIGENCE SUMMARY.
(Erase heading not required.)

Place	Date	Hour	Summary of Events and Information	Remarks and references to Appendices
Front line CARENCY	17.9.16	6.30p.m.	Gun fire and the explosion of one of our mines. Casualties four wounded.	
"	18.9.16	6.30p.m.	Hostile trench mortars very active. A mine was successfully exploded at 1.39 a.m. doing considerable damage to enemy's sap, also causing portion of our front line to collapse, damage being repaired before daylight.	
"	19.9.16	8.30p.m.	Regt. relieved from the line and proceeded to billets at VILLERS AU BOIS.	
VILLERS AU BOIS	18.9.16	"	Battalion bathed; each man being issued with clean socks and shirt. Weather rainy.	
"	19.9.16	"	Parades under Coy arrangements. No change. Wet weather.	
"	20.9.16	"	Relieved 3rd S.R. in front line. Trenches in bad condition.	
CARENCY front line	21.9.16	"	Enemy very quiet. MINENWERFER active, doing no damage.	
"	22.9.16	"	Enemy quiet. Relieved by 13th Middlesex, and proceeded to CAMBLAIN	
CAMBLAIN L'ABBE	23.9.16	"	L'ABBE.	

114

Army Form C. 2118.

WAR DIARY
or
INTELLIGENCE SUMMARY.
(Erase heading not required.)

Place	Date	Hour	Summary of Events and Information	Remarks and references to Appendices
BERTHONSART	24.9.16	8.30p	Regt. proceeded to BERTHONSART – distance 5 miles.	
MAIZIERES	25.9.16	"	" " " MAIZIERES – " 12 "	
"	26.9.16	"	No change.	
"	27.9.16	"	Training carried out in Divisional Training area.	
"	28.9.16	"	No change	
GRAND RULLECOURT	29.9.16	"	Regt. proceeded to G. RULLECOURT to be nearer training area – distance 5 miles. Roads very muddy.	
"	30.9.16	"	Company training carried out.	

General
Sir Haig
Comdg. P.F.S A 9

WAR DIARY or INTELLIGENCE SUMMARY.

Vol 3 — 1st Bn S. Staffordshire

Place	Date	Hour	Summary of Events and Information	Remarks and references to Appendices
GRAND RULLECOURT	1	6.30 pm	No change	
"	2	"	— do —	
"	3	10 am	— do —	
"	4	10 am	— do —	
"	5	10 am	25 men sent for attachment to 2B Machine Gun Coy.	
			Regiment marched to BONNIÈRES — distance 11 miles.	
BONNIÈRES	6	10 am	No change	
LAHOUSSOYE	7	10 am	Battalion travelled to LAHOUSSOYE by motor Buses. Weather wet.	
MAMETZ WOOD	8	10 am	Battalion marched to HINER HILL and then travelled by trucks on railway reaching MAMETZ WOOD after dark. Officers and men slept in shelters and dugouts.	
BAZENTIN- LE GRAND	9	10 am	Batln moved to BAZENTIN LE GRAND occupying the old system of trenches which the men had to sleep in.	
"	10	10 am	General fatigues and salvage work. A large quantity of brass shells 18 pdr cartridge cases, rifles steel, men packs and stores were salved.	

Army Form C. 2118.

WAR DIARY
or
INTELLIGENCE SUMMARY.
(Erase heading not required.)

Place	Date	Hour	Summary of Events and Information	Remarks and references to Appendices
MILLENCOURT	25th	6.30pm	Divs. detachment moved to MILLENCOURT - distance 3 miles	
"	26/9	"	No change	
"	27/9	"	Road-repairing party reported regiment	
REBEMPRE	28/9	"	Bttn moved to REBEMPRE - distance about 5 miles	
DUISANS	29/9	"	Moved by motor buses to DUISANS	
"	30/9	"	No change	
"	3/10/16	"	No change	

J Saunders
Lt-Col
Comdg 9th R. Sussex Regt
3/10/16

WAR DIARY or INTELLIGENCE SUMMARY.

Army Form C. 2118.

Place	Date	Hour	Summary of Events and Information	Remarks and references to Appendices
BAZENTIN LE GRAND	11/10/16	5.30pm	No change.	
HIGH WOOD	12/10/16	"	Moved into High Wood - taking over from the 2nd S.R.?	
STAR FISH TRENCH	13/10/16	"	Moved to STAR FISH TRENCH.	
"	14/10/16	"	No change.	
"	15/10/16	"	Party of 100 sent to front line to act as stretcher bearers	
"	16/10/16	"	- do -	
FRONT LINE EAUCOURT L'ABBE	17/10/16	"	Report on Operations ~~~~~ already submitted.	
"	18/10/16	"	Relieved from front line during early hours of morning	
"	19/10/16	"	No change	
HIGH WOOD	20/10/16	"	- do -	
BAZENTIN LE GRAND	21/10/16	"		
"	22/10/16	"	Moved to MAMETZ WOOD.	
MAMETZ WOOD	23/10/16	"	350 Officers and men moved to FRICOURT FARM for employment on road repairing. The remainder of Battalion with H.Qrs. proceeded to ALBERT.	
ALBERT	24/10/16	"		

SAB.Conf.15/O.

1st South African Infantry Regiment,
24th October 1916.

Sir,
I have the honour to report as follows on the recent Operations.

On the night of the 16th/17th OCTOBER I took over the Sector of trenches on the left of the 26th BRIGADE from the 3rd S.A.I.

Having been informed by the Brigadier that my Regiment would attack the enemy's trenches on the following night and been given the general lines on which the attack would be conducted I had drawn up provisional orders (marked "A" and attached) and gone through them with my Company Commanders.

On the morning of the 17th I took the Company Commanders round the trenches, pointing out to each the objective, line to consolidate, strong points and limits of his company front. I emphasized the necessity of every Officer, N.C.O. and man having these objects pointed out to him and knowing exactly where to go and what to do. This, I have ascertained, was done.

Later in the day the operation orders were received from the Brigade which rendered certain amendments necessary. These were issued and sent round. Copies attached marked AI and A2.

During the early part of the night rain fell which made the trenches and parapet very slippery. The front line trench was deep: and narrow, without fire bays or fire steps except some which had been made the previous night. The Trench was a new one.

Recognising the difficulty of getting the men out , the Company Commanders commenced to form their men up on the alignment, upwards of an hour before ZERO.

At ZERO A and B Companies had about half a platoon each still in the trenches, C Company's men being all on the alignment. The three companies less the men in the trenches started off up to time and kept as close to the barrage as possible. "C" Company passed the C.T. leading from the PIMPLE to the SWITCH trench and arrived in front of the SWITCH TRENCH. Here however they were held up in some places by wire at the foot of a steep bank in front of the GERMAN trench and were very heavily BOMBED from the trench. The leading Platoon was shot down with the exception of four men and though an Officer and about six men of the second platoon managed to get into the GERMAN trench, they were immediately shot down as were many others. The only Officer left was Captain JENKIN'S who was himself wounded and that Officer seeing that the Germans trench was strongly held and that there was no hope of his remaining men capturing it, ordered the Company Sergeant Major to take the men back to our orginal line. The Casualties of this Company were 69 out of about 100 who went over the Parapet.

From subsequent reports it appears that "A" and "B" Coys. reached their Objective,- Captain WHITING, Commanding "B" Company being mortally wounded half way across,-but failed to recognise their objective and continued to advance. With the exception of a few stragglers and the carrying platoons nothing more has been seen of these two Companies. 2nd/Lieutenant STAPLETON of "B" Comapny was one of those who returned, shooting some ten GERMANS and capturing 19 on his way in. His report is attached and marked "B".

I should mention that about 90% of the rifles were clogged with mud.

At daybreak on the 18th the situation was therefore as follows :- "C" Company was known to have failed, the whereabouts of "A" and "B" were not known but from reports from wounded it was believed they had attained their objective. They could not be seen in " NO MAN'S LAND".

At attempt was now made to BOMB along the trench leading to the SWITCH from the PIMPLE, but this broke down under the fire of the Machine guns in the SWITCH which enfiladed the C.T. At 9 am. a notification was received to this effect from Major ORMISTON in the PIMPLE stating that if Artillery or STOKES MORTAR fire could be brought to bear, the bombing party might be able to do something.

I then sent Major ORMISTON orders not to proceed with the BOMBING until further orders.

In the meantime a Company of the 3rd S.A.I. under Captain LANGDALE had been ordered up from the SUPPORT LINE to our FRONT LINE TRENCH, a Company of the 4th S.A.I. being sent to replace them in the SUPPORT LINE.

At 9.35 am. I sent the following instructions to Captain LANGDALE :-

"Position not yet cleared up with reference "A" and "B" Companies. Prisoners have been brought in from captured trench and you must send out a patrol to ascertain position and on receipt of their report send one platoon forward to establish themselves in GERMAN TRENCH. The two men who acted as escort to these GERMAN PRISONERS will be instructed to report to you on return and you can utilise them as guides."

This was followed by a second message at 10. am.,

"Guides referred to in previous wire will not be available for some hours but you can get 2nd/Lieutenant STAPLETON "B" who knows the route used. If possible the whole of your Company should be sent forward. If you are unable to get hold of Lieutenant STAPLETON strike due NORTH of PEARSES strong point."

The following replies were received to these at 1.20 pm.& 4.30 pm

(1) My Company is now in front line PEARSES TRENCH and 4th are occupying SUPPORT TRENCH 12.25. Patrol not yet returned.

(2) The whole of my Company is in PEARSES TRENCH - Officers patrol has returned and has been unable to obtain information from Lieutenant STAPLETON or any one in the Ist Regiment. I have however just seen the C.S.M. of "C" Coy. and he has pointed out the place he is almost certain is the trench held by "A" and "B" Companies. If this is the right place it is impossible to get into communication by day without without being under heavy rifle fire or machine gun fire from the BOSCH trench. It could be done I think at night. Awaiting your further instructions

During the whole of the 18th I was endeavouring to get artillery and two-inch T.M. fire on the NOSE of the SWITCH M.17.c.4.5. instead of M.17.c.I.8 where the artillery was firing. The Artillery Liaison Officer Lieutenant WEBB repeatedly asked for it. I also saw Captain LAIDMAN and asked him to do his best to open fire on this point with the two-inch T.Ms.

Instructions had been received that an attack was to be made on the SWITCH at 5.45 pm. if it was not taken earlier and that there would be artillery preparation.

At 12.50 pm. I sent the following message to Major ORMISTON.

" "A" Company is in touch with 26TH BRIGADE in enemy's Trench we are not sure where "B" Company is but some men are undoubtedly in touch with "A". The idea now is to BOMB the SWITCH trench and junction with Artillery, two-inch T.Ms. and STOKES until a given hour when you are to rush bombers through. Two or three men first and then a large number, as many as necessary. I am in touch with the T.M.Battery. Are you in touch with Stokes gun yet ? Do you think we could arrange to start the bomb attack at 4.pm.? Come and see me if necessary, and let me have any suggestions you may wish to make."

Finding it was impossible to organise this attack for 4.pm I issued orders as follows :-

(1) T.Ms to fire at M.17.c.4.4 until 5.40 pm. Stokes to open fire at 5.40 pm for two minutes. "D" Company to attack along trench from PIMPLE at 5.45 pm or immediately Stokes Guns cease fire. One Company of 3rd Regiment to attack from the SOUTH at the same time. Artillery to switch to M.17.c.I.8 at 5.40 pm.

(2) O/C.SCOTTISH. Send one platoon from the S.P. in valley on WEST to reinforce the Company at the PIMPLE. O/C."D" Coy. of Ist S.A.I will provide guide. Only one platoon to be left in S.P. in valley.

(3) CAPTAIN LANGDALE. The Ist S.A.I. is attacking the NOSE from the PIMPLE. You will attack at the same time from

(3)   You will attack at the same time from the SOUTH, in
three or four lines, whichever you prefer. "A" and "B" Coys
1st S.A.I. have a footing in the enemy trench about M.17.
c.7.5 but the exact point is not known. Our Artillery
will be firing on the NOSE of the SWITCH and the trench
until 5.40 pm. The Stokes guns will fire from 5.40 to
5.42 pm. You should advance at 5.42 pm.

At 6, 7.34 and 7.45 pm I received messages from Major ORMISTON to say that his BOMBING attack had started as arranged although there was no preparation by artillery or two inch Mortars. The Stokes guns had fired as arranged. The attack had failed, very few of the bombers getting back. Major ORMISTON and I agreed that it was essential to attack this point from the EAST. It was and is my opinion only one well directed shell on point M.17.c.4.5 was required to render the capture of this point and with it the whole switch trench an easy matter.

At 7.53 pm I sent Lieutenant FARMER to enter the GERMAN trench captured by the 26th BRIGADE, follow it to the WEST and ascertain the position. He returned later, time not noted, and reported that there were only about 10 of our men on the left of the 26th BRIGADE.

Between 9 and 10 pm. Captain LANGDALE, 3rd S.A.I. reported to me verbally that he had taken up his men to the GERMAN trench to support the attack carried out by "D" Company., 1st S.A.I,. He told me that he had entered the trench and proceeded along it to within 25 yards of the SWITCH, where he had seen two or three GERMAN MACHINE GUNS. He had not however attacked them, but had withdrawn his men to our front line where they then were. I at once told him that he should not have left the German trench and gave him peremptory orders to reoccupy it immediately. He stated that the men were very tired and it would take a long time to turn them out. I repeated the order and he went away to carry it out.

At 10.5 pm. I sent him the following order :-
" G.O.C. says you are to reoccupy the German trench immediately
notifying me by this orderly as soon as you have done so.
FOUR Vickers Guns will then be sent up. Captain ROSS with
120 men are coming up tonight and will attack the strong
point at the corner. If he is unsuccessful you will be
relieved before dawn, but if successful you will not be re -
lieved before tomorrow night. The reason for this is that
if unsuccessful the strong point will be shelled tomorrow in
which event only a few men will be in the trench to hold it.
Send over a platoon to reoccupy it just as soon as you can
get ready. Dont wait until the whole Company is ready."

These orders were sent on the instructions of the G.O.C.BRIGADE.
From this time until we were relieved on the night of the 19th/20th Major ORMISTON kept a BOMBING party in the PIMPLE ready to attack the SWITCH directly he saw an attack approaching from the EAST.

At 1.am on the 19th a message was received from Captain LANGDALE, 3rd S.A.I. to the effect he had reoccupied the SNAG trench. Captain ROSS and 120 men of the 4th S.A.I. had also gone forward to occupy this trench and attack the SWITCH but up to 7.am. had not reported their arrival. At 5.am Major ORMISTON observed a FLAMMENWERFER attack to be in progress against our men in the SNAG from the SWITCH trench and sent in a report to this effect. Artillery support was asked for.

At about 7.am a telephone message was received from the 26th BRIGADE to the effect that the SOUTH AFRICANS and BLACK WATCH were retiring to their original front line. A runner was despatched to MAJOR ORMISTON asking if he would give any information and at about 8 am the following message was received in reply :- " As previously reported by messenger enemy attacked towards portion of trench at nose of SWITCH about 300 yards EAST. From report they appear to have used flame fire. As soon as reported I had Vickers and Lewis guns put on them. About 20 minutes later we could see numbers of them retiring along same direction as they advanced. We accelerated their progress. NOSE appears crowded with men but they made no direct effective against us. There was no artillery support from our side though I called for it twice, and our people on right did so repeatedly. Have sent to find number of effectives in my Company but approximately it is only about 50 men here. These are badly shaken up and I should judge unfit for attack. The constant strain and exposure has been very great. The platoon

(4)

The platoon of 4th Regiment consists of 10 men and I Officer. Situation is now quiet at this spot. Artillery fire on NOSE of SWITCH trench badly required. Enemy is shelling PIMPLE intermittently

No message was received from either Captain LANGDALE, 3rd S.A.I. or Captain ROSS, 4th S.A.I,.

At 10.20 am an URGENT message was received asking for artillery support on the SWITCH and SNAG trench up to a point 300 yards EAST of the junction. At the same time Captain LANGDALE, 3rd S.A.I. arrived at my BATTALION HEADQUARTERS and reported as follows :-

"He had advanced along the SNAG trench to a point about 25 yards from the SWITCH, when he was attacked with FLAMMENWERFER and BOMBS, being driven back a short distance, and a Lewis gun and two rifles being burnt. The attack however made no further progress and he held his ground until the arrival of Captain ROSS and 120 men of the 4th S.A.I. who then took over his position. In accordance with his orders he then withdrew to our original front line. I would here point out that this action was contrary to the written instructions given him by me."

He further stated -

"That immediately he began to move the Germans attacked him in rear but without success. They then made an encircling movement to the N.E. and attacked his right flank. I am not clear as to what happened then but Captain LANGDALE stated that the 4th S.A.I. were in position and did not appear to be hard pressed."

I had barely finished interrogating Captain LANGDALE when Lt. HAY, 4th S.A.I. arrived and reported that he was the only Officer left of Captain ROSS' party, that he had only 20 men with him all of whom were back in our original front line, the other three Officer being Casualties.

Information was shortly afterwards received to the effect that a few of the 3rd and 4th S.A.I. were on the left flank of the 26th BRIGADE and that the Bombing attack had ceased.

The SNAG trench could be effectively enfiladed from the PIMPLE though it was difficult to see whether the occupants were our men or the enemy for more than about 100 yards EAST of the SWITCH.

Throughout the 19th however it was known that they were Germans and a continuous machine gun and Lewis Gun fire was kept on the trench. Our artillery was also firing, the F.A. especialist making excellent practice. It frequently happened that small bodies of the enemy, unable to stand the strain any longer, got out of the trench and bolted across the open towards the BUTTE. Very few of them however managed to get away. Our Snipers had some excellent shooting, the best Sniper in the Regt. firing upwards of 390 rounds.

This continued throughout the day until only a very few of the enemy were left in the SNAG. The Machine guns were however still at the junction, untouched by our artillery fire and pro- tected from our Machine Guns.

At about Noon Lieut. ELLIOTT, 3rd S.A.I. reported at Battalion Headquarters for instructions, having been sent by the G.O.C. BRIGADE. I put a Map before him and explained the situation fully and gave him verbal orders to take his men into the new C.T. leading from our front line to a point 75 yards south of the German line and to endeavour to cross and occupy the latter. If however the hostile M.G. fire from the junction of the SWITCH and SNAG trenches were effective, he was not to persist until the M.Gs. had been silenced. Having arrived at the German Trench, he was to get in touch with the 26th BRIGADE and then bomb his way along the SNAG and the SWITCH up to M.17.c.18. where a Bombing block was to be established. I further told him that 2nd/Lieutenant HALLACK would support him and occupy the SNAG behind him as he proceeded and would provide him with Bombs.

I particularly mentioned that I did not think he would meet with much opposition and that in my opinion the most difficult part of the Operation was getting into the German Trench from the C.T. I informed him that Major ORMISTON at the PIMPLE had a party ready to co-operate directly he approached the junction.

Lieutenant NICHOLSON, 1st S.A.I. and 2nd/Lieutenant VAN RYNEVELD 3rd S.A.I. were present when I gave these instructions. I went ove

(5)

I went over them twice. Lieut. ELLIOTT asked several questions and then at my request repeated them to me. He said that he had no Map and I therefore gave him one. He then left me and I sent out the necessary orders to Major ORMISTON and 2nd/Lieutenant HALLACK.

Shortly afterwards in consequence of telephone instructions from BRIGADE HEADQUARTERS I sent several written messages to Lieut. ELLIOTT pointing out the URGENCY of proceeding immediately. I also informed him that the Germans were evacuating the SNAG trench. These messages are in his possession.

At 2.55 pm Lieutenant ELLIOTT entered the German Trench without difficulty. Immediately he had done so he ordered Lieut. HALLACK, 1st S.A.I. to support him and take up Bombs. Lieutenant HALLACK complied taking up 6 or 8 boxes in addition to the 2 bombs per man, and notified Lieutenant ELLIOTT that he had done so. Instead of being put in the EASTERN part of the trench he was ordered to go between two platoons of Lieutenant ELLIOTT'S party.

I was informed from an outside source at 3.5 pm. that this party had gone over but had no further information up till about 5.30 or 6 pm. when three runners arrived in quick succession with verbal messages which left no doubt in my mind that the SNAG and SWITCH trenches had been taken. I interrogated one or two of the messengers personally and one of them stated that if they had some supports and more bombs they could get on to the BUTTE. I immediately notified BRIGADE HEADQUARTERS and sent a written message to Lieut. ELLIOTT not to go beyond the SWITCH trench and to establish a block at M.17.c.Ø. I.8. The only copy of this message is in possession of Lieut. ELLIOTT. Some of the messengers stated that our shells were falling among our men and asked for the artillery fire to be lifted. Colonel CONNELL had now arrived to take over.

All previous messengers from the German front line and that vicinity had taken about an hour to get through. I also knew that our artillery were firing on point M.17.c.4.5 but did not know they were firing to the EAST of this point. At 8.pm I received a message as follows :-

"FROM MAJOR ORMISTON - Situation is now as follows. About 4.35 pm parties of our men were able to get into German trench at point approximately 300 yards EAST of NOSE. But they made no attempt to bomb towards NOSE, though I had a party ready to effect junction as soon as this was done. I could not pass the block in CROSS trench owing to SNIPERS still at NOSE. They are still there & appear to have been reinforced by small parties, therefore still hold SWITCH and I cannot get across. It is vital that people in trench E of NOSE bomb down to NOSE. Enemy front line lightly held at SWITCH and strongly at 2nd line"

I notified BRIGADE HEADQUARTERS immediately and sent Lieutenant FARMER, 1st S.A.I. to clear up the situation and if he found that Lieut. ELLIOTT had not proceeded he was to give him peremptory orders to attack immediately. No further information was obtainable until 2 am when Lieut. FARMER who had been delayed by the mud returned and informed me that Lieutenant ELLIOTT had not pushed forward at all. He had therefore delivered my message and Lieutenant ELLIOTT had replied he had done his best, but could get no further. He had sufficient bombs to repel an attack but not to advance.

One Company of the K.O.S.Bs (The 6th) had already gone forward to occupy the SNAG trench. My runners were completely exhausted and the state of the trenches was such that I did not think further action on my part was possible. I therefore put the full facts of the case before Brigade Headquarters and Lieut. Colonel CONNELL of the 6th K.O.S.Bs., and on completion of the relief early on the morning of the 20th I returned to HIGH WOOD.

Throughout these Operations we were very greatly handicapped by the mud. M.Gs, L.Gs. and rifles were continually jamming, and in the case of rifles they were so bad that the men could not clean them. On the night of 19th/20th there was not a M.G., L.G., or rifle in the PIMPLE that could be fired. On the 19th the mud in the C.T. was in no place less deep than 18 inches and in many places it was 3 feet.

The men were extremely exhausted from the mental strain, the exertion of getting through the mud and from exposure. It was continually necessary to dig some of them out, and several remained in the mud all night through inability to extricate themselves. If a man was wounded in the trenches and not rescued quickly he became suffocated in the mud. Eight and sometimes ten men were necessary to carry a Stretcher.

On getting out there was not a single rifle that could be fired. I may mention that every man brought a rifle and equipment out with him.

In conclusion I would like to draw attention to the excellent work done by Major ORMISTON, not only in making the SNAG trench untenable but in keeping me as closely informed of everything that occurred, as was possible under the circumstances.

I much regret that I failed to complete the task allotted to me by the G. O. C.

I have the honour to be,

Sir,

Your obedient Servant,

(Sd) F.S.DAWSON, Lieut-Col.
Commanding 3rd S.A.Infantry Regiment,.

"A"

PROVISIONAL OPERATION ORDERS.

1. The 1st S.A.I. will attack the enemy's front line trench at ZERO on the ....instant.

2. At ZERO - 30 A., B., and "C" Companies less carrying platoons will be drawn up in our front line trench "A" being on the right "B" in the centre and "C" on the left.
   Two platoons of "D" Company will hold the mound and trench
X. at M.16.d.9.3. The remaining two platoons of "D" Company will be in the trench connecting with the 15 DIVISION.
   The three carrying Platoons will be in the new C. T. leading to the PIMPLE.

3. At ZERO - 15 the right platoon of each Company will crawl over the parapet and form up in line immediately in front of our wire covering the whole of the Objective.

4. Directly they are in position, this line will crawl forward the centre platoons will do the same, following the first at such a distance as to keep them in sight, but not exceeding 70 yards. The left platoons will follow in a similar manner.

5. When the barrage lifts, the three lines will rise and advance in quick time to the enemy's trench.
   Each platoon will march by its centre a N.C.O. being detailed to direct, having been shown a point to march on by daylight.

6. The front line will jump in the enemy's trench and deal with any of the enemy found therein. It will Bomb but not enter dugouts and will leave a sentry at the door of each and over prisoners
   It will then advance from 200 to 300 yards further, " C" Coy clearing the SWITCH trench as far as the pit.
   Each platoon of this line will then establish a post consisting of two Sections and one Lewis Gun at places which will be pointed out to the platoon Commanders.
   All the men of the platoons in question will assist in the consolidation of these posts, except those detailed as covering party.

7. The 2nd line will advance to a position which will be pointed out to it about......yards in front of the enemy trench and will proceed to dig itself in from the SWITCH trench on the EAST to that on the WEST.

8. The 3rd line will clear the enemy's trench including dugouts, sending back all prisoners and handing them over to " D " Coy. at about M.17.c.I.3.
   It will then join the 2nd line and assist in the consolidation being primarily responsible for the wiring. The men not so employed will dig.

9. The Company Commanders and Lewis Gunners will advance to the 3rd line. On reaching the Objective, Company Commanders will immediately notify "D" Company.

10. On receiving the message as in 9 - O/C."D" Company will send the carrier platoons forward finding any additional carriers required and notifying Battalion Headquarters.

11. Lieutenant NICHOLSON will be responsible for a sufficient quantity of Bombs and S.A.A. being sent up to the new line and advanced posts.

12. The REGIMENTAL Dump will be at M.16.d.9.3.

(2)

13. The M/Officer will make arrangements for the evacuation of Wounded.

14. Greatcoats will be dumped under Company arrangements and sent forward by carriers as opportunity offers.

15. All Officers, N.C.Os. and men must know before-hand exactly what they are going to do.

16. The 26th BRIGADE will be Operating on our right and will bomb up the trench running N.W. from M.17.d,3.6. The O/C. "A" Company is responsible that touch is kept.

17. BATTALION HEADQUARTERS will be at M.22.d.3.2 and the O/C. "D" Company will maintain the service of runners from the PIMPLE to BATTALION HEADQUARTERS.

18. All communication with the rear will be along the captured trench to the PIMPLE and new C.T. leading SOUTH there-from unless the hostile barrage permits direct communication across country.

****

"A"

"AMENDMENTS TO ORDERS."

1. The line to be consolidated will be enemy's present line but the advanced platoons will form strong points at suitable spots in front thereof as in previous orders excepting that - "A" Company advanced S.P. will not be in trench taken by 26th BRIGADE but to the WEST thereof.

2. "C" Company will take the SWITCH trench as far as M.17.c. 1.8 and will hold it. If there is not sufficient space for the whole Company the rear platoon will occupy part of the trench to the EAST of the junction with the SWITCH trench.

3. "D" and "C" Company Commanders will make some arrangements together to obviate the possibility of firing into or bombing one another,.

4. As previously arranged the 2nd line will dig and the 3rd wire.

5. A Company carrying platoon will be in the trench leading SOUTH from PEARSES S.P. instead of in the PIMPLE trench.

6. Artillery barrage on front line will last one minute and will then recede by lifts of 50 yards a half minute. The STOKES will barrage the front line for one minute after the Artilery. A Company less carrying platoon will be in the portion of the trench allotted to it by 2 am. By this time the carrying platoons must also be in position. "C" Company will be clear of its trench by 2 am. to enable "B" to file in to its position. "C" Company will take up its position as soon as "B" is in its position.

"A.2."

ZERO is at 3.40 am. Artillery barrage will be from 3.40 to 3.41 and will then go back in lifts of 50 yards every half-minute. Stokes guns will barrage enemy's trench from 3.41 to 3.42 and during this minute the first wave should approach fairly close to trench. During this second minute Artillery barrage will be 50 and 100 yards in re trench.

****

(II)

127

I think therefore that a considerable length of the enemy's trench was not covered and that it was thus that I became cut off.
I enclose rough sketch giving approximately the ground covered and directions taken.

(Sd) P.H.STAPLETON, 2/Lieut.
1st S.A.Infantry Regiment.
22/10/1916.

"B"

At 1 am on the 18th OCTOBER, 1916 "B" Company, 1st S.A.I. left the MILL. The orders for the attack had been explained by CAPTAIN WHITING to the platoon Commanders who were taken to view the ground in front of PEARSES S.P. and these orders were as carefully explained by them to the N.C.Os and men.

I was in Command of No.8.Platoon with orders to form the Centre of the 2nd wave of the attacking force. A Platoon of "A" Company being on my right and one from "C" Company on my left. I issued orders to my right and left Sections to connect with the inner flank of "A" and "C" Companies respectively.

Owing to the extremely narrow trench between the MILL and PEARSES S.P. the Company had great difficulty in reaching its pre-arranged jumping off point. Furthermore the trench was very wet and slippery and the men could not mount the parapet except at one point where it had been damaged. This meant that little if any time was left to us to organize the arranged formation for the attack. In fact the order to advance came before all the men of the 3rd wave had left the trench.

The attacking line advanced fairly rapidly behind our barrage in spite of the broken and sodden condition of the ground.

On arrival at what I took to be our Objective I ordered the men in my vicinity to dig in. What I concluded to be the trench at this point was so battered about by shell fire that it had lost all semblance of a trench.

I now saw that the line which by this time had lost all Formation was advancing on my right and left so I presumed that we had not yet reached our Objective. I therefore gave the order to advance.

After advancing about 200 yards I came up to the remainder of the attacking force which I found to be digging in under 2nd Lieutenants O'KEEFE and BUDGEN and to consist of about equal proportions of "A" and "B" Companies.

I told 2nd/Lieut. O'KEEFE to carry on whilst I endeavoured to establish communication on our left with "C" Company. I reconnoitered to the WEST and reached the SWITCH trench which I found to be strongly held by the enemy who was engaging in the opposite direction,-S.W. I then realised that "C" Company had not gained its Objective and that we "A" and "B" Companies had passed over ours. I returned to where I had left 2nd/Lieutenant O'KEEFE but found that he and his party had gone, I picked up one straggler of "B" Company and six of "A" Company and moved in a SOUTH-EASTERLY direction. I found a trench taped out and partly dug which I knew to be in existance some distance N. of our Objective. I decided to remain there until there was sufficient light to enable me to size up the situation.

I saw enemy stragglers moving off in a N.E. direction. Only two of the rifles and my revolver were in working order. With these we managed to account for several - at least 10 - of the enemy. One of the enemy bumped into the trench near us and we made him Prisoner. As the light improved we took several more.

With a pair of field-glasses I was able to find the enemy front line between me and PEARSES S.P,. This was still fairly strongly occupied. On the crest of the rise, about 600 yards E.I saw a party of our men - apparently HIGHLANDERS with a few other men. About midway between us was a party of enemy. I signalled to the party on the rise that I would join them and was proceeding thence when I saw them return and disappear from the sight at the double. I then decided to try and make my way back to PEARSES S.P. over the gap in the enemy trench - In doing so we were fired on by a party of the enemy at the end of the Sap leading S.S.W. from the SWITCH, in the NOSE of which I saw a Machine Gun. One of my men was killed and five of them took refuge in shell holes and came in that night. I managed to get through with one man and nineteen prisoners.

I am of opinion that "A" Company wheeled towards the BUTTE and thus lost touch with the line on the right. The right section of my platoon, to whom I gave orders to extend to the right until they connected up with "A" Company did so but found no one of "A" Company and eventually joined up with the CAMERONS.

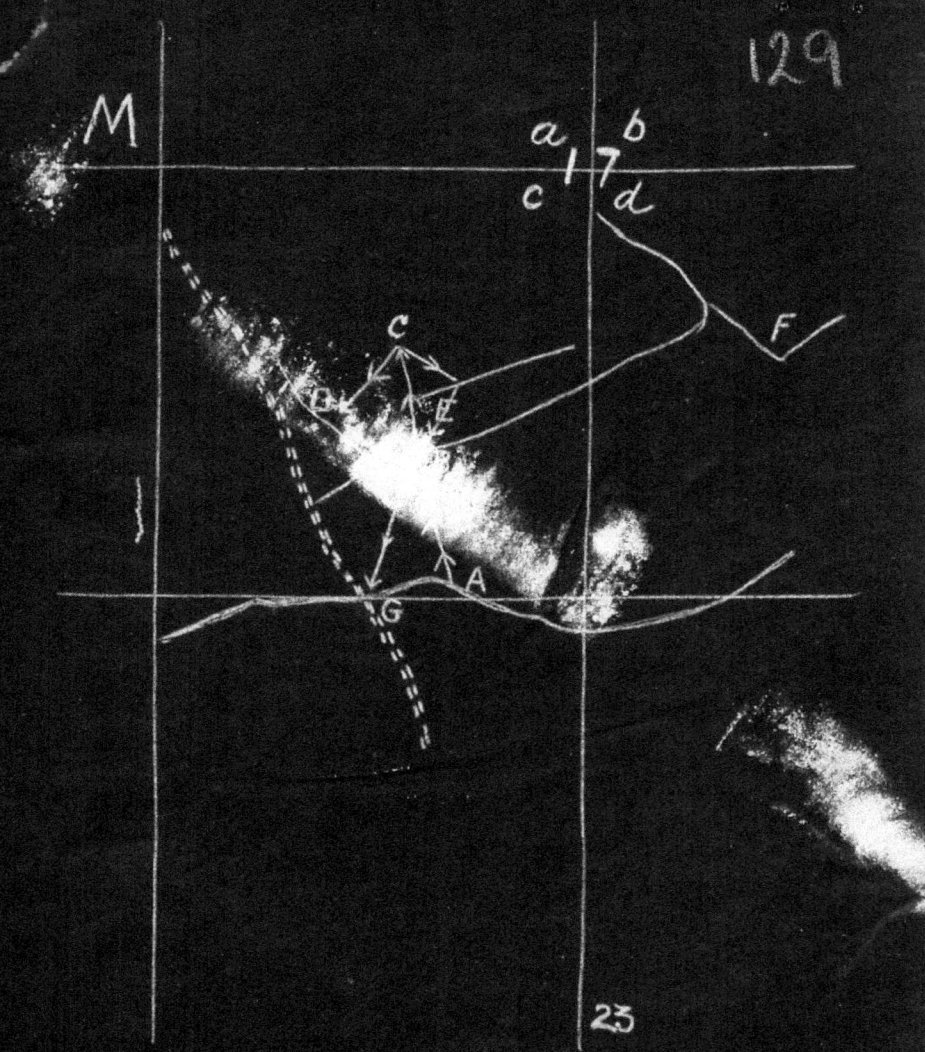

A- Point of exit- Jumping off point
B- Point where objective was crossed.
C- Point where Lt. O'Keefe was left
D- Point reconnoitered
E- Point held until retirement
F- Point where Scottish party was seen
G- point of re-entry.

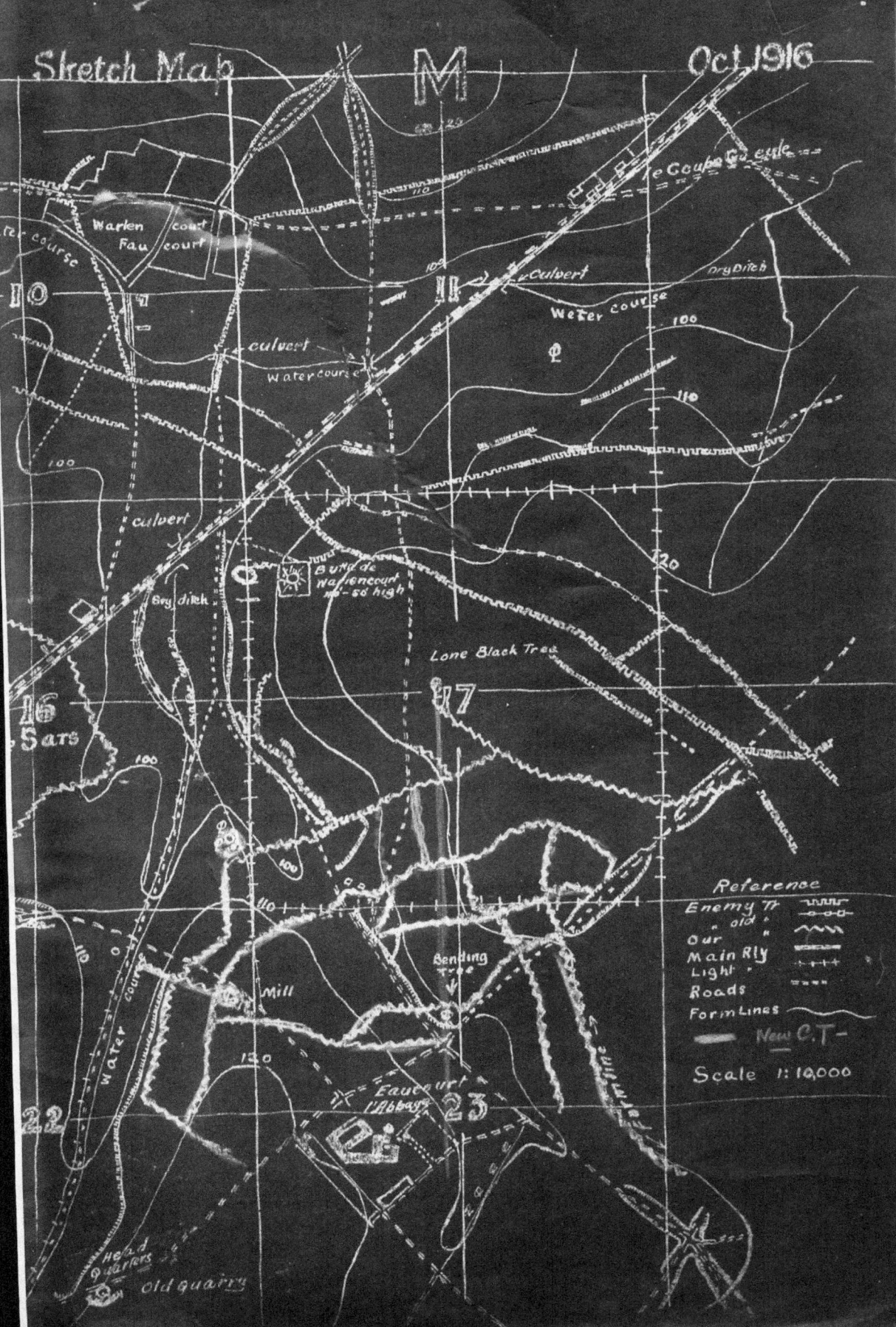

WAR DIARY
or
INTELLIGENCE SUMMARY.

Army Form C. 2118.

1st South African M.G.C

VOL 8

Place	Date	Hour	Summary of Events and Information	Remarks and references to Appendices
DUISANS	1/11/16	8:30pm	New draft from Gun Class of 4 Officers and 144 men commenced Parades under Coy arrangements from 9 to 12.30 pm	The L.G. Classes were postponed without previous recognition of being run
"	2/11/16	"	— do —	Coy. Parade for speed training Bayonet fighting Squad arms goals & drill
"	3/11/16	"	— do — Subalterns	
"	4/11/16	"	Paraded at 2.30 pm Luncheon Parades under Coy Arrangements 9 - 12.30 pm	
"	5/11/16	"	Church Services. Subalterns Parade 9 – 12.30 pm	
"	6/11/16	"	Coy Parades 9 – 12.30 pm from Gun class of 4 offrs and 144 men commenced	Company Parades Physical training Bayonet fighting Platoon drill & musketry
"	7/11/16	"	Draft of 54 arrived from Base. Parades – 9 - 12.30 pm men Coy arrangements. Subalterns – 9 to 12.30 pm during afternoon.	Section training Subalterns Classes
"	8/11/16	"	Parades under Coy Arrangements 9 - 12.30 pm. Subalterns 9.12.30 pm	Draft from Base Parade on Commander's Squadrill under armed Coy commanders drill
"	9/11/16	"	Parades:- Coy Arrangements 9-12.30. Subalterns 9 to 12.30 pm Route march 2 – 4 pm.	V31
"	10/11/16	"	Parades – Coy Arrangements 9.12.20 Subalterns "Compass Marching" 9 am	

WAR DIARY
or
INTELLIGENCE SUMMARY.
(Erase heading not required.)

Army Form C. 2118.

Place	Date	Hour	Summary of Events and Information	Remarks and references to Appendices
DUISANS	11/2/16	6.30pm	Third Lewis Gun Class of Officers and N.C. men commenced.	
"	12/2/16	"	Parades 9-12.30 am. Coy training. Subalterns 10.30 am Church Services.	
"	13/2/16	"	Bayonet Fathers. 2 companies bathed.	Company Parade
"	14/2/16	"	Parades. Company training 9 to 12.30 pm. Night training 5.45-6.45pm	Passed Bayonet fighting Squad names drill
"	15/2/16	"	Remainder of Regt. bathed. Company training 9 to 12.30 pm. Subalterns parade 10.30 to 12.30 pm Recreational training in afternoon.	Bombing with dummy grenades musing
"	16/2/16	"	Company training 9 to 12.30 pm. Subalterns 10.30 to 12.30 pm Night training 5.45 to 6.45 pm. Rugby football in afternoon.	Subalterns do A new Map Reading Class Arms drill
"	17/2/16	"	Company training 9 to 12.30 pm. Subalterns 10.30 to 12.30 pm — do —	Squad drill in live rounds
"	18/2/16	"	— do —	
"	19/2/16	"	Church Parade 9am.	Night operations
"	20/2/16	"	Parades under Coy Arrangements. 9 to 12.30 am. — do —	Night attack practice with
"	21/2/16	"	practice 5.45 to 6.45 pm night attack	Company arrangements

132

Army Form C. 2118.

WAR DIARY or INTELLIGENCE SUMMARY.

(Erase heading not required.)

Place	Date	Hour	Summary of Events and Information	Remarks and references to Appendices
BULSCAMP	22/4/16	8.30pm	9.12.30 pm. Company training. Breakfast training during afternoon.	Company parades. Physical training. Bayonet fighting. Bombing with dummy & live grenades.
"	23/4/16		9-12.30 pm Training. One Company practised with live grenades. 5.45 to 6.45 pm night operations.	Squad morse drill (mainly responsibility)
"	24/9/16		9 to 12.30 training. football played in afternoon. One company practised in live grenade throwing and field engineering. 2 pm Battalion paper chase. All available officers and men attended.	Fire engineering. Respirator training. Daily NCO's instruction
"	25/9/16		Lewis Gun Class assembled 9-12.30 training. Recreational training in afternoon.	
"	26/9/16		Box respirators tested by gas NCO with shell gas in small hut. Every available officer, NCO and man was put through test. Church parade 9am.	Company parades in morning. St Luke's feast day was observed as Christmas and Stampery 4 officers Shamers noon mass Monday thereof.
"	27/9/16		9 to 12.30pm training. 10.30 am tactical scheme for officers and NCOs. 5.45 to 6.45 pm night operations.	
"	28/9/16		Training 9am to 1pm. Inter platoon route march competition in afternoon.	Bat. NCO's map reading class
"	29/9/16		Training 9am to 1pm. Rugby football in afternoon.	

133

Army Form C. 2118.

WAR DIARY
or
INTELLIGENCE SUMMARY.
(Erase heading not required.)

Place	Date	Hour	Summary of Events and Information	Remarks and references to Appendices
BUIRE-SUR-ANCRE	29/11/16	8.30 am	Training 9 to 1 pm. Intensive digging, close order, arms drill, bayonet fighting, box respirators drill. Rehearsed training consisting of bombing and wiring platoon today. ace [20 men per platoon].	

R. Bousfield
Captain & Major
Cmdg. 1st Batn. A.I.F.
1/12/16
(tenth advent meeting)

134

WAR DIARY or INTELLIGENCE SUMMARY

1st South African Infantry

Army Form C. 2118.

Place	Date	Hour	Summary of Events and Information	Remarks and references to Appendices
DU SANS	1/2/16	8.30pm	Parades. Training under Coy arrangements. Bayonet fighting, close order drill, intensive digging, hip firing with live rounds, arms drill, musketry. NCOs map reading class 9-10am. Stretcher bearer class 10.30 - 12.30 pm.	
"	2/2/16	"	Parades - Training under Coy arrangements.	
Front line ARRAS - 2nd section JI	3/2/16	"	Took over front line from 16 Batt⁵ Cheshire Regt. Day was very quiet.	
"	4/2/16	"	Hostile aeroplanes active several crossing the line during the morning. Enemy TMs were fairly active during the afternoon.	
"	5/2/16	"	Quiet day.	
"	6/2/16	"	Quiet day. 2 men killed and two wounded by hostile TM in front line	
"	7/2/16	"	Our artillery active.	
"	8/2/16	"	Quiet day.	
"	9/2/16	"	Quiet day.	
"	10/2/16	"	Enemy TMs active during day. 1 man wounded by enemy aerial torpedo.	

WAR DIARY or INTELLIGENCE SUMMARY

1st Bn Infantry

Place	Date	Hour	Summary of Events and Information	Remarks
Front line ARRAS 1st Sub-sector	11/12/16	8.30pm	Enemy T.Ms did considerable damage to support line. Several heavy shells were sent over to our rear - damage unknown. Four enemy planes crossed the lines during the morning. They were subjected to a heavy fire. Three lights were sent up from enemy lines at 7-10pm. These lights burst up about 6 differently coloured lights. Nothing occurred after these went up. Two officer patrols were out but owing to unfavourable light, little could be done.	
12/12/16			Our artillery shoot provoked hostile retaliation with T.Ms. No damage done.	
13/12/16			Enemy T.Ms did some damage to FEBRUARY AVE. Night quiet. Bad weather has done considerable damage to our trenches necessitating much work.	
14/12/16			Hostile artillery fairly active. No damage resulted.	
15/12/16			Hostile T.Ms active. Our artillery and T.Ms bombarded enemy trenches and wire. Results could not be observed. Enemy quiet.	

WAR DIARY

Army Form C. 2118.

137

Place	Date	Hour	Summary of Events and Information	Remarks and references to Appendices
Front line ARRAS J1 Sub-section	16/2/18	1.30pm	Enemy quiet, our TMs exploded near MARCH AV. doing no damage. Aircraft very active. At 8.45 am an enemy plane flying low fired a few rounds at a party of men near the Baths? Cookhouse without effect. Five enemy planes steeple patrolled our lines and three of them attacked a machine of ours but failed to bring it down. Our artillery was quiet.	
"	17/2/18		A few TMs were fired at our front line without effect during the morning. After a bombardment of the enemy line and wire, he retaliated with heavy and light TMs, aerial torpedoes and small calibre shells. Little damage was done to our trenches. Usual patrols were out at night. A salvage party of 1 officer & quantity of wire in No Mans Land. Enemy artillery was comparatively quiet during 2 hours. Our TMs effected considerable damage to enemy wire.	
"	18/2/18		Enemy TMs active during afternoon causing damage to FEB AV. and A wks. Hostile patrol heard at midnight and was fired on by our Lewis Guns. Our TMs were active during afternoon, effect not observed. Usual patrols went out.	

Army Form C. 2118.

WAR DIARY
or
INTELLIGENCE SUMMARY.
(Erase heading not required.)

Place	Date	Hour	Summary of Events and Information	Remarks and references to Appendices
ARRAS Front Line ARRAS — II Sub-section	20/2/16	6.30pm	Usual working parties supplied.	
	21/12/16		Relieved 4th Saltrg in line. Quiet day. Trenches in bad condition due to wet weather.	

P Ogminton
Major
Comdg 1er Sqt.

138

WAR DIARY or INTELLIGENCE SUMMARY

Army Form C. 2118.

139 END

Place	Date	Hour	Summary of Events and Information	Remarks and references to Appendices
Front Line ARRAS – F1 Sub-section	21/12/16	1.35pm	Enemy Artillery inactive. An enemy patrol was heard during the night but could not be located. Our LTMs registered several hits on enemy trench.	
"	22/12/16		Hostile TMG fairly active – no damage done.	
"	23/12/16		Quiet. The usual patrols were out during the night. The regiment was relieved on by the line by 4th SAI and moved into billets in ARRAS. Two platoons of "A" Coy moved into FORESTER REDOUBT to garrison it.	
ARRAS.	24/12/16		No change.	
"	25/12/16		Working parties of 200 men provided for work in trenches.	
"	26/12/16		Usual working parties supplied.	
"	27/12/16		Usual working parties supplied. Commencing at about 10 p.m. the enemy sent several thousand gas shells into the town. The effects are not known.	
"	28/12/16		Usual working parties supplied.	
"	29/12/16		Usual working parties supplied.	

9TH (SCOTTISH) DIVISION
SOUTH AFRICAN INFY BDE.

1ST STH AFRICAN INFY REGT

JAN - DEC 1917

9TH (SCOTTISH) DIVISION
SOUTH AFRICAN INFY BDE.

9TH DIVISION
S.A. INFY BRIGADE

10

S.A. INFY 1917

9TH DIVISION
S.A. INFY BRIGADE

Army Form C. 2118.

WAR DIARY
or
INTELLIGENCE SUMMARY. 1st South African Infantry Regt.
(Erase heading not required.)

Instructions regarding War Diaries and Intelligence Summaries are contained in F.S. Regs., Part II. and the Staff Manual respectively. Title pages will be prepared in manuscript.

Place	Date	Hour	Summary of Events and Information	Remarks and references to Appendices
ARRAS Front Line T.I. Sub-Section	1/1/17	5.30pm	Enemy quiet.	Vol (1)
	2/1/17		Enemy sent a few 77mm shells into our lines. No damage done. Patrol went out to examine enemy wire.	Officers
"	3/1/17		Our artillery and L.T.M's active during the day on enemy front trench. Enemy wire examined during night and found very strong.	
"	4/1/17		Enemy sent over a few 77mm shells now and again during the day. Early in evening enemy sent up green and red lights. No action followed.	
"	5/1/17		Enemy sent gas shells towards town between 10.45 and 11.30 pm. Enemy aeroplane driven back over town on lines at 10am. Our LTM's shell German front line. No patrols out during night.	
"	6/1/17		Enemy sent gas shells over during night. Hostile T.M's shelled our trenches. During the day German aircraft twice attempted to cross our lines but were driven back. Our artillery was quiet.	
"	7/1/17		During afternoon enemy heavily shelled our lines with 77mm and 5.9' shells. Hostile heavy T.M's also in action.	
	8/1/17		Quiet. Our artillery had a "shot" on enemy lines. Results not observable.	

WAR DIARY
INTELLIGENCE SUMMARY. 1/5 Welsh.

Army Form C. 2118.

Place	Date	Hour	Summary of Events and Information	Remarks and references to Appendices
ARRAS	10/11/17	2.30 pm	Enemy slightly shelled our line. No damage.	
"	11/11/17		Enemy mining party dispersed by Lewis gun fire during night. Hostile heavy TMs damages our front line but examined enemy wire which was found to be good.	
"	12/11/17		Hostile heavy TMs active. Our TMs fired on enemy wire doing considerable damage. Officers patrol went over during night and found two gaps in the wire.	
"	13/11/17		Hostile TMs damage trench 63. Our TMs active during the day, damaging enemy wire. No hostile movement observed during post 21 hours.	
"	14/11/17		Quiet. Hostile party, about 30 strong, seen on road behind enemy lines.	
"	15/11/17		Enemy fire on a few MGs on our lines during morning. Enemy put up moderate barrage, during which they sent up numerous red rockets between 8.30 pm and 9 pm.	

Army Form C. 2118.

WAR DIARY
or
INTELLIGENCE SUMMARY.
4,
1st Battalion
(Erase heading not required.)

Place	Date	Hour	Summary of Events and Information	Remarks and references to Appendices
ARRAS	23/1/17	8.30pm	line and proceeded to billets in ARRAS	
"	24/1/17	"	No change	
"	25/1/17	"	Working parties (2 offrs and 2 over 200 other ranks) supplied.	
"	26/1/17	"	—do—	
"	27/1/17	"	—do—	
"	28/1/17	"	—do—	
"	29/1/17	"	—do—	
"	30/1/17	"	—do—	
"	31/1/17	"	—do—	

Signed
LIEUT. COLONEL
COMMANDING 1st S.A. INFANTRY

Army Form C. 2118.

WAR DIARY
or
INTELLIGENCE SUMMARY.
(Erase heading not required.)

Instructions regarding War Diaries and Intelligence Summaries are contained in F. S. Regs., Part II. and the Staff Manual respectively. Title pages will be prepared in manuscript.

Place	Date	Hour	Summary of Events and Information	Remarks and references to Appendices
ARRAS Front line T.1. Sub-section	17/1/17	8.30p	Enemy artillery and TMs shelled our line during afternoon. During night an enemy party was discovered laying but was driven off by R.G. fire.	14
"	18/1/17	"	Enemy seems more alert and aggressive. It is probable that a relief has taken place.	
"	19/1/17	"	Enemy sent over a few heavy shrapnel shells doing little damage. During the evening sounds of enemy transport were heard.	
"	20/1/17	"	Quiet.	
"	21/1/17	"	Enemy artillery and TMs very active doing damage to portion of our front line. Our heavy TM fired 12 shells damaging enemy wire and trenches.	
"	22/1/17	"	Hostile TMs active during day causing a little damage. Two pigeons flew over our line from ARRAS. A heavy explosion was heard near a hostile heavy TM emplacement. It was not caused by our shells. The battalion was relieved out of the	
"	23/1/17	"	Enemy artillery active.	

WAR DIARY
or
INTELLIGENCE SUMMARY. 1st South African Infantry.

Army Form C. 2118.

Place	Date	Hour	Summary of Events and Information	Remarks and references to Appendices
Subsection TRONES-FRONT LINE A.	1/2/17	6.30pm	Relieved 1st South African Infantry in front line.	
	2/2/17		Quiet day. Hostile TMs fairly active during afternoon.	
	3/2/17		Hostile field artillery active during the day. Our Heavy TM active in afternoon.	
	4/2/17		Enemy fired about ten 5.9 shells on our front line. Hostile TMs were active during the day.	
	5/2/17		Quiet day.	
	6/2/17		A few hostile TMs were fired on our line.	
	7/2/17		Hostile TMs very active. Enemy aggressive. There seems to have taken place from enemy to change of attitude a relief appears to have taken place.	
	8/2/17		Enemy TMs active. Our MGs fired on PARROTS BEAK with good effect. No patrols or emplacements. Our artillery fired on "Thinnenefer" during the night.	
	9/2/17		Enemy M.T.M.s active. Enemy patrol dispersed during the night. Hostile artillery active on right. No damage done.	
	10/2/17		Our Heavy TM put out of action at 2pm by 4.2 shell. Our Artillery	5

WAR DIARY
INTELLIGENCE SUMMARY — 1st South African Infantry

Army Form C. 2118.

Place	Date	Hour	Summary of Events and Information	Remarks and references to Appendices
T.Subsector ARRAS front line	1/2/17	8.30 p	Quiet. Our heavy TMs fired on enemy's line during much damage. No patrols were out during the night.	
"	2/2/17	"	Enemy sent a few trench mortar shells & a light TM shells in our front line doing slight damage. Aircraft of both sides very active. One enemy machine was seen to fall in his lines. At 9pm the Germans sent over 12 shells which burst into light lights. Our field guns fired a few salvoes on enemy front line. Usual hostile TM activity. Our heavy light and medium TMs fired on enemy lines with apparent good results. Apparently was prepared by Sap 91. A patrol of 1 offr, Capt Robertson & the Gloucesters had previously seen A patrol of 1 offr and 4 Ranks left Sap. 91. for the purpose of examining enemy wire. A gap was found in the wire evidently caused by our TMs. The patrol proceeded through the gap and when enemy parapet Pte Forsch fired 6 shots at sentries who appeared and Sgt Brampton fired three shots. The enemy opened fire	
"	3/2/17	"		

WAR DIARY
INTELLIGENCE SUMMARY: 1st South African Infy.

Army Form C. 2118.

Place	Date	Hour	Summary of Events and Information	Remarks
Bp I Schen Rl Sola PARAS FRONT LINE	14/2/17	6.30 p.m	with rifles and MGs. Patrol returned safely. Officer in charge of party is certain that two of the enemy were killed by Pte FORSCH-	17
"	"	"	A few light and heavy shells were fired on our lines during the morning. Our field guns retaliated on Minenwerfer emplacements during the day. Some of [illegible] which had begun travelling was driven behind enemy lines. Our snipers drew on hit opposite Sap.81.	
"	15/2/17	"	Our Medium TMs fired about 30 shells at 2.30 p.m. The Medium TMs replied with about 16 HTm shells and 8 LTM shells damaging trench 84. An enemy wiring party was dispersed during the night by our L.G. fire. 3 Officers patrols were out. One	
"	16/2/17	"	was caught by M.G. fire and casualties resulted. 2Lt McKENZIE was brought in wounded but Ptes ROSS and PHILLIPS are missing.	
"	17/2/17	"	Our artillery was active during the day. Hostile MGs were very active during night which prevented officers patrol which endeavoured to locate missing men from effecting its purpose.	

Army Form C. 2118.

WAR DIARY
or
INTELLIGENCE SUMMARY. 1st South African Infy.

(Erase heading not required.)

Instructions regarding War Diaries and Intelligence Summaries are contained in F. S. Regs., Part II. and the Staff Manual respectively. Title pages will be prepared in manuscript.

Place	Date	Hour	Summary of Events and Information	Remarks and references to Appendices
No 1 Section Lt Section Beaurains ARRAS Support Line	19/2/17	7.30pm	Moved into Brigade Support, 3rd S.A.I. taking over front line. 2nd Lt. Phillips who was wounded in NO MANS LAND on night 18th was brought in by 3rd Regt.	
"	19/2/17		Working parties of 200 men supplied. Trenches in very bad condition owing to thaw.	
"	20/2/17	"	No change.	
"	21/2/17	"	No change.	
"	22/2/17	"	No change.	
"	23/2/17	"	No change.	
"	24/2/17	"	No change.	
"	25/2/17	"	No change.	
No 1 Section Lt Section Front Line ARRAS	26/2/17	"	Relieved 3rd S.A.I. in front line. Enemy artillery very active.	
	27/2/17	"	The Battalion carried out a raid on enemy front line between points G.18.c.27.15 and G.18.c.28.14., with the following objects:— (a) To capture prisoners—dead or alive.	08

T1134. W: W708–776. 500000. 4/15. Sir J. C. & S.

WAR DIARY or INTELLIGENCE SUMMARY. 5/-

Army Form C. 2118.

(b) to do as much harm to the enemy as possible. The party comprised 2 officers and 50 other ranks equally divided into Right and Left columns. The party crossed NO MAN'S LAND without being discovered and the guides reached enemy wire before Stokes Guns minute barrage opened - were able to locate enemy working party. The artillery barrage opened sharp at 7.10pm. just as the leading men of the two columns reached enemy lines. Within a few minutes the enemy artillery had started to shell his own front line 7.7 m.m. shells OILWORKS and REDOUBT LINE with 4.2o and 5.9o. Enemy M.G. enfilades FEBY and ROAD to ST NICHOLAS. The left column encountered two Germans who ran away in the approach of our men, one was killed and shoulder strap and button cut off. Another German was found in a shell-hole and killed by a bomb. Two of the enemy working party were killed, probably by the Stokes fire. The enemy trenches were in a battered condition, depth about 10 feet, width about 5 to 6 feet.

Every man appeared to have known his work, and carried

WAR DIARY
or
INTELLIGENCE SUMMARY.
(Erase heading not required.)

Army Form C. 2118.

Place	Date	Hour	Summary of Events and Information	Remarks and references to Appendices
			it out without confusion or hesitation and in silence throughout. One man was killed and four other ranks slightly wounded during the operation. As a result of the operation the raiders have acquired great confidence in our artillery barrage. The fire of the artillery and TMs. was exceedingly accurate and well-timed throughout.	
No Section	27/1/17		Quiet day. Our field guns fired on enemy front line; effect not observed.	

Sgd.
LIEUT. COLONEL
COMMANDING 1st S.A. INFANTRY.

WAR DIARY or INTELLIGENCE SUMMARY

Army Form C. 2118.

1st South African Infy.

Place	Date	Hour	Summary of Events and Information	Remarks and references to Appendices
Front line Areas Mk N°1 Sect. Pt Sdn	1/3/17	8.30pm	Hostile artillery active during day. A few shells fell near support line	
"	2/3/17		No change	
"	3/3/17		Hostile artillery and T.Ms active.	
Y Huts WEETRUN	4/3/17		Relieved out of line by 1st Seaforth Highlanders and proceeded to training area.	
"	5/3/17		Battalion was inspected by Field Marshal Sir Douglas Haig, who expressed his appreciation on the turn out of the two Regts inspected (1st and 4th SAI) which he considered extremely creditable under the circumstances.	
"	6/3/17		Company training	
"	7/3/17		Company training	
"	8/3/17		Company training	
"	9/3/17		Company training	
"	10/3/17		Training – minor operations by Coys.	
"	11/3/17		Company training in morning. Battalion was inspected by	

WAR DIARY
INTELLIGENCE SUMMARY

Army Form C. 2118.

Place	Date	Hour	Summary of Events and Information	Remarks and references to Appendices
			The Secretary of State for Colonies (Rt Hon. Walter Long) in the afternoon, who afterwards expressed his appreciation of the excellent turn out of those Regts of this Brigade which he inspected, and informed the Brigadier-General Commanding that he would notify His Majesty the King of the satisfactory state of the Brigade.	
MONCHY-BRETON	12/3/17	5pm	Battalion moved to new training area.	
"	13/3/17	"	Company training in training ground.	
"	14/3/17	"	Training under Coy:- Close order drill; physical training; attack in artillery formation; Bombing and Rifle Grenade Training. Bayonet Fighting.	
"	15/3/17	"	-do- -do-	
"	16/3/17	"	Training - Battalion in attack (day and night practice).	
"	17/3/17	"	Training - Battalion in attack under the Commdg. Officer.	
"	18/3/17	"	Company - minor operations in morning and Battalion attack practice (night works).	
"	19/3/17	"	Company - training - minor operations	

WAR DIARY or INTELLIGENCE SUMMARY.

Army Form C. 2118.

Place	Date	Hour	Summary of Events and Information	Remarks and references to Appendices
MONCHY-BRETON	20/3/17	8.30pm	Training – Brigade attack scheme.	
"	21/3/17	"	" Minor manoeuvres by platoons	
HERMAVILLE HAUTE AVESNES	22/3/17	"	Battalion moved to new area.	
"	23/3/17	"	Working parties supplied for work on range and artillery Remainder: Physical training, bayonet fighting and extended order drill.	
PENIN	24/3/17	"	Battalion moved to PENIN.	
"	25/3/17	"	Training – Minor Operations – morning; Recreation – afternoon.	
"	26/3/17	"	" "	
"	27/3/17	"	" "	
"	28/3/17	"	2 Coys moved to ARRAS as working parties for artillery and head-Quarter Batteries. Remainder Coy training in morning and recreational training in afternoon.	
"	29/3/17	"	A & B Coys training	
"	30/3/17	"	A & B Coys & HQrs moved to Y Huttments, W. ETRUN.	
"	31/3/17	"	Company training –	

_____ LIEUT. COLONEL
COMMANDING 1st S.A. INFANTRY.

WAR DIARY South African Infantry

Army Form C. 2118.

Vol 73

INTELLIGENCE SUMMARY.

Place	Date	Hour	Summary of Events and Information	Remarks and References to Appendices
Y HUTMENTS NEAR ETRUN	1/4/17	6.30pm	Company Training 9am – 4.30pm	
"	2/4/17	"	–do–	
"	3/4/17	"	Battalion moved into line and took over Brigade sector for the attack ie. between points G.18.b.5.8. and G.12.c.7.8. Our artillery heavily shelled points in enemy front and rear systems. Enemy reply mainly directed on front and support trenches.	
"	4/4/17	"	Special Coy. R.E. discharged gas over enemy trenches with Livens Gas Projectors and 4" Stokes Shells at 6.15 am. Preliminary Bombardment commenced at 6.30 am. Enemy shelled front and support trenches chiefly with 5.9s and 7.7 mm. Casualties 4 killed and 8 wounded.	
"	5/4/17	"	Bombardment maintained. Enemy retaliation not heavy. Gas discharges. Our artillery practised creeping barrage. Casualties 1 Killed 1 Died of Wounds 7 wounded.	
"	6/4/17	"	Bombardment in progress. Gas discharged on enemy trenches. Creeping barrage practised by artillery.	

WAR DIARY (3)
INTELLIGENCE SUMMARY

Army Form C. 2118.
1st South African Infy.

Place	Date	Hour	Summary of Events and Information	Remarks and references to Appendices
Billets ARRAS	8/4/17	7.30 pm	returning to our lines at 3.15 pm with 3 prisoners of 6th Company 6th Bavarian Regt, 14th Bavarian Division. The identification obtained were very important. Dugouts were bombed and several Germans believed shot. As a result of the raid all ranks obtained a greater confidence as to the efficiency of our artillery barrage. Casualties during raid 1 killed & 3 wounded. Battalion relieved at nightfall by 3rd S.A.I.	
	9/4/17		Day spent in issuing stores, etc.	
Trenches	10/4/17	8.30 pm	Battalion moved up to concentration area at 11/30 pm 9/4/17 ready for the attack on the German trenches which commenced at 5.30 A.M. — see annexure "A".	
"	11/4/17	"	See Annexure "B".	
Support line	12/4/17	"	In support line to 26th Infty Brigade.	
"	13/4/17	"	—do—	
"	14/4/17	"	Casualties 1 other rank killed 2 oRanks wounded	

WAR DIARY
1st South African Infantry
INTELLIGENCE SUMMARY

Army Form C. 2118.

Place	Date	Hour	Summary of Events and Information	Remarks and references to Appendices
TRENCHES	6/4/17	2.30pm	During the night our artillery lifted on enemy support lines and a patrol of 1 officer and 16 Ranks attempted to enter enemy trenches for the purpose of obtaining identification. The patrol was seen by enemy when 40 yards from his trench and heavily fired on by M.G.s and artillery causing casualties. Patrol was forced to return, bringing in wounded. Casualties (2) Died of wounds and 3 wounded.	
"	7/4/17		Bombardment still in progress. Gas discharges and heavy wire cutting. Barrage practices. Identifications were urgently needed on the Corps front and it was decided to carry out a daylight raid on the enemy trenches between points G.12.c.5.5. 2 and G.c.l.4.5. for the purpose of obtaining such information. The party was divided into three columns consisting of (1) Blocking party (2) Clearing party and a small reserve — total strength 5 officers 50 other ranks. Zero was at 3pm and the party reached the German trench without a casualty —	

WAR DIARY

Army Form C. 2118.

1st South African Infantry

(Erase heading not required.)

Place	Date	Hour	Summary of Events and Information	Remarks and references to Appendices
ARRAS HUTMENTS PL9	15/4/17	8.30pm	Relieved in support line by 51st Division at dusk.	
	16/4/17	"	Moved to hutments south of ARQ, arriving at 4.30 pm	
"	17/4/17	"	Day spent in re-organizing companies.	
"	18/4/17	"	—do— two companies bathed	
"	19/4/17	"	Reorganizing. Remainder of Battalion bathed.	
"	20/4/17	"	No change.	
"	21/4/17	"	Battalion moved to LA THIEULOYE.	
LA THIEULOYE	22/4/17	"	Companies at disposal of Coy Comdrs; attention being paid to the cleaning of equipment etc.	
"	23/4/17	"	Training - Lewis gun classes and Recruits.	
"	24/4/17	"	No change	
"	25/4/17	"	Parade Requiem Service for the dead. Afternoon - Recreational	
"	26/4/17	"	Physical training, Close Order and Arms drill Ceremonial drill, Lewis Gun and Signalling Classes. 9-12.30pm & Afternoon - Regimental and football.	
"	27/4/17	"	No change	

Army Form C. 2118.

WAR DIARY
or
INTELLIGENCE SUMMARY. 1st South African Infantry.

(Erase heading not required.)

28

Place	Date	Hour	Summary of Events and Information	Remarks and references to Appendices
A. THIEPVAL	28/4/17	8.30p		
	29/4/17	"	No change. Church Services in morning.	
	30/4/17	"	Physical training, Close Order and Arms Drill; Rapid loading, Fire Discipline; Indication of Targets and judging Distances. Extended Order Drill. 9 – 12:30 P.m. Afternoon– recreational.	

Lipkal
Lieut-Col-
Comdg 1st Regt S.a.Infy.

were dropped at 12-41 and at 12-45 p.m. we advanced well up with the barrage. Up to this point all wire in our sector had been thoroughly demolished but on east side of road running H.8.b.8.5 to H.8.d.7.0 there was a thick broad belt of wire which had not been touched by artillery. Had there been any resistance the Battalion could only have negotiated this obstacle after heavy casualties. This wire was crossed by the lanes used by the enemy and the BROWN LINE was reached where prisoners of the 26th WURT. REGT. of ARTILLERY were captured together with one or two M.Gs. and a lot of artillery materiel. After our barrage had lifted off the BROWN LINE one of our guns still continued to fire on LAUREL TRENCH.

Parties of the enemy were seen running away from CAR and EFFIE TRENCHES minus equipment, arms etc. Lewis Guns were opened on them. A shot from one of our guns caused several casualties, including two officers at the BROWN LINE. During the occupation of the BROWN LINE our barrage died down to occasional shells and several small parties of the enemy took this opportunity to come in and surrender.

The 4th Division moved up and took over, continuing the advance to the GREEN LINE, and on relief by their Reserve BRIGADE the Battalion withdrew.

The enemy offered no resistance after the BLUE and was completely demoralized.

Our barrage throughout was magnificent and the men advanced close up to it quite fearlessly. Our total casualties for the day were 5 Officers and 80 other ranks.

We saw no evidence of our M.G. barrage.

The 4th Division might have caused confusion by moving up to the valley west of the BLUE LINE from the south before this Battalion had passed through, but the training of the men overcame this difficulty.

C.C."A" Coy (Capt.KIRKHAM) reported to me that a man of the 2nd Regt. had been blown up by a mine of some sort which appeared to go off when he trod on a wire.

Lieut-Colonel,
Comdg. 1st Regt. South Afr. Infantry.

1st South African Infantry Regt.,
18/4/17.

SOUTH AFRICAN BRIGADE.
_____

OPERATIONS ON 9th APRIL, 1917.

Battalion were in position by 2 am. on night 8/9th April. We suffered practically no casualties before Zero although enemy shelled our old front line very heavily for about an hour and then intermittent with 4.7s. Enemy started single sniping shots from about 4-45 am, accompanied by flares, and evidently became suspicious for at Zero minus four minutes he put up an SOS signal, but I cannot say how long it took for his artillery to reply.

Our artillery opened at ZERO and leading battalions moved out accompanied by the MOPPERS UP. I should like to state that the work of Mopping Up, combined with the advance later on the BROWN LINE, was too heavy a strain on the men concerned, both officers detailed by this unit collapsed at the end of the day and had to be relieved.

Enemy artillery replied to our barrage by placing a heavy fire of all calibre guns on our own and their front system of trenches.

In comparison with remainder of the operations our casualties among the Moppers Up were severe.

We occupied the BLACK LINE when leading Battalions captured the BLUE LINE. An enemy M.G. firing from south of the SCARPE worried us during the halt in this position causing several casualties.

Company Commanders report that during the advance to BLUE LINE the flanks became slightly intermingled, a good fault. This was not noticeable after advance from BLUE ~~BLACK~~ LINE although touch was maintained throughout.

At 11-45 am. the leading companies moved out of sunken road to the valley west of the BLUE LINE preparatory to attacking the BROWN LINE. This move was carried out in excellent order and at 12-30 pm. we passed through the outposts of the 2rd and 4th Regiments and halted. The smoke shells were...

The extreme point of advance reached by this unit was the first German Trench in H.18.d. where they were held up by the heavy Machine Gun fire, and by this time had suffered severe casualties.

The left of our line finished up rather in rear of the right company and dug in. Lewis Guns were brought into action against hostile Machine Guns with results unknown. The enemy artillery barraged the infantry as they advanced with a very accurate fire. Positions of hostile machine guns as far as it was possible to locate them have already been advised you.

At 8-15 pm. the advanced line withdrew to our original front line, the 4th Division then withdrew their men from the trench near the railway embankment.

The regiment was relieved during the course of the night by the 26th Brigade.

The enemy made no concerted attempt to counter-attack but several small parties left their trenches and took up other positions, probably to obtain better field of fire. Some fifty of them attempted to work down the C.T. running west from ROEUX ROAD through I.13.a., H.18.b. This party was driven back by Lewis Gun fire from "A" Company on the left.

The Officer in Charge of a company of the Duke Of Wellington's W.R.Regt, FAMPOUX, informed me on arrival in the village that they had not been advised of any attack being made that afternoon, but merely that they would be relieved that evening.

I consider that the behaviour of the men throughout was beyond all praise.

Arnkal

Lieut-Colonel,
Comdg. 1st Regt. S.A. Infantry.

10/4/17.

1st South African Infantry Regt.,
10/4/17.

SOUTH AFRICAN BRIGADE.
OPERATIONS OF 12TH APRIL, 1917.

The Brigade was ordered to attack the road running north from ROEUX through CHEMICAL WORKS. The objective for this Battalion was from STATION inclusive to a point about H.7.c.8.8. ZERO was at 5 pm on 12th April.

At 3 pm. we moved out of our position in EFFIE TRENCH due south to the ATHIES-FAMPOUX ROAD at H.16.d.4.5 and thence east along the said road to our assembly position in FAMPOUX. This movement was carried out in file with intervals between companies but was undoubtedly observed by the enemy. At about 3-45 pm I received an order that this unit was not to be used. The Battalion was reported in position at 4 pm.

At about this hour the enemy opened up a heavy barrage on FAMPOUX causing several casualties, and the roads running east from the village were enfiladed by M.Gs. At about 4-45 pm the leading left company reported that they were unable to leave the shelter of the houses owing to the heavy M.G. fire and I ordered them to remain until ZERO and then push forward and catch up the barrage. The right leading company was able to work forward into position under cover.

A very thin barrage opened at 5 pm. The right company commander advised me that the barrage opened in rear and to the left of his men and that he drew his men close to the railway embankment running east along the right of our line of advance. The barrage then appears to have jumped to the small wood in H.16.d. and the second jump 100 yards further on. The fourth jump carried the barrage to the edge of the station buildings. Immediately the barrage passed our leading line the men started the follow up, but it travelled much too fast and they were quite unable to keep up with it. The shelling on the embankment was just missing it and falling on the south side and in consequence the machine guns in the embankment were not touched. There did not appear to be many "Heavies" falling on the CANDLE WORKS and STATION.

The ...

INTELLIGENCE SUMMARY. 1st South African Infantry.

(Erase heading not required.)

Instructions regarding War Diaries and Intelligence Summaries are contained in F.S. Regs., Part II. and the Staff Manual respectively. Title pages will be prepared in manuscript.

9th/4

Place	Date	Hour	Summary of Events and Information	Remarks and references to Appendices
LA THIEULOYE	1/5/17	5.30 pm	Training—	
"	2/5/17		Physical, Close Order and Arms Drill, Rapid Loading, Fire Control and Fire Discipline, Indication of Targets and Judging Distances, Extended Order drill. 9—12.30 pm. Cricket and Recreational Training afternoon	
"	3/5/17		No change	
"	4/5/17		Training under Company arrangements 9—12.30 pm. Lewis Gun Instruction for Officers. 9.30—12.30 pm. Recreational in afternoon	
"	5/5/17		—do—	
"	6/5/17		Composite Company of 4 Officers and 119 of Ranks with four Lewis Guns, sent to ARRAS. for duty.	
"	7/5/17		Church Parade.	
"	8/5/17		Draft of 12 other ranks joined battalion. All training— Lewis Gun instruction - all Coys 9—12.30 am. Officers Riding Class. 6.55 am.	3
"	9/5/17		Inspection of draft by Cmdg Officer. 9am. Lewis Gun instruction all Coys 9—12.30 am.	4

1577 Wt. W10791/1773 500,000 1/15 D.D. & L. A.D.S.S./Forms/C. 2118.

WAR DIARY (3)
or
INTELLIGENCE SUMMARY

Army Form C. 2118.

1st South African Infantry

Place	Date	Hour	Summary of Events and Information	Remarks and references to Appendices
LA THIEULOYE	17/5/17		Bayonet fighting, Musketry, Arms Drill, etc. 9-12 noon. Recreational – 2-4.30 P.M.	
"	18/5/17		Musketry, Extended Order Work, Bombing, Lewis Gun Instruction, Signalling and Scouting. 7-12 noon.	
"	19/5/17		Training as for 17th	
"	20/5/17		Musketry and firing at range at Monchy Breton. Section training	
"	21/5/17		Sunday – Church parades.	
"	22/5/17		Training on training ground – Bombing, musketry, bayonet fighting. 8-12 noon.	
"	23/5/17		Do. for 21st.	
"	24/5/17		Training – Physical training, Arms and Squad Drill. 9-10 A.M. 1-1.15 P.M. Attack practice during daylight and after dark carried out.	
"	25/5/17		8-12 noon Company training. No change.	

33

WAR DIARY

Army Form C. 2118.

1st South African Infantry

Place	Date	Hour	Summary of Events and Information	Remarks and references to Appendices
LA THIEULOYE	10/5/17		Training:- Lewis Gun Instruction. all Coys. 9-12.30 PM. Officers Riding Class 6.55 AM.	
"	11/5/17		Training - Lewis Gun Instruction 9-12.30 PM. Bearer Class 10-12.30 PM. Officers Riding Class 6.55 AM. Sketches	
"	12/5/17		Training under Coy arrangements Lewis Gun Instruction.	
"	13/5/17		10 am Battalion inspected by Army Commander (with other Regiments of the Brigade). After the inspection the Army Commander expressed his appreciation of the smart and clean turn out of the men. 8.45 am. Lewis Gun Course fired at range at training ground by Officers and other ranks who had not previously fired this course. Remainder employed at training under Company arrangements.	
"	14/5/17		Training on training ground:- Lewis Gun Instr., Signalling. Starting at Musketry. 9-12.30 AM. from ARRAS. Composite Coy returned to Regt.	35
"	15/5/17		Training:- Musketry and Physical Drill 6.30-7.30 AM. Bombing	

Army Form C. 2118.

WAR DIARY
or
INTELLIGENCE SUMMARY.
(Erase heading not required.)

1st South African Infantry

Place	Date	Hour	Summary of Events and Information	Remarks and references to Appendices
ATHIEULOYE	26/5/17		Brigade Sports were held at Monchy-Breton having ground.	
"	27/5/17		Church services in morning. Musketry - firing at rifle range 12:30 to 5 pm.	
"	28/5/17		Training 8-30 - 9.30am. Arms and Squad drill. 6.15am. Battalion attack practice carried out during daylight and after dark.	
"	29/5/17		Training under Coy arrangements from 6-30 to 7-30 am and 9 - 12 noon. Subalterns parade 7 - 8 am. Lecture to NCOs 6 - 7 pm.	
"	30/5/17		Presentation of rebands by Corps Commander to following Officers, NCOs and Men:-	
			MILITARY CROSS. Lieut T.C.SCHEEPERS Capt. G.ROODT	
			DISTINGUISHED CONDUCT MEDAL:- 9089 Sgt. T.STAFFORD	
			MILITARY MEDAL:- 536 Cpl. E CARTER, 5152 Pte PEARCE W.C, 3563 Pte W. CAYMAN.	
			9572 L/Cpl CLARKE W.W	
"	31/5/17		"A" & "D" Coys proceeded to ARRAS for employment with 17th Tunnelling Coy. Remainder parades under Coy. arrangements.	3

Army Form C. 2118.

WAR DIARY

of ~~INTELLIGENCE SUMMARY~~ 1st South African (4)

(Erase heading not required.)

Instructions regarding War Diaries and Intelligence
Summaries are contained in F. S. Regs., Part II.
and the Staff Manual respectively. Title pages
will be prepared in manuscript.

37

Place	Date	Hour	Summary of Events and Information	Appx
Y Huts	29/6/17		Raining.	
"	29/6/17		Training from 6-30 to 7.30 AM and 8.30 to 1 P.M. under Coy arrangements.	

Signed
LIEUT. COLONEL.
COMMANDING 1st S.A. INFANTRY.

WAR DIARY

Army Form C. 2118.

1st South African Infantry

Place	Date	Hour	Summary of Events and Information	Remarks and references to Appendices
Y Huts Nr ETKIN	18/6/17		Training:- 6 to 7.30 AM; 8 to 11 AM, 1 - 4 PM. Firing at rifle range; Lewis Gun Instruction; Swedish drill; Musketry; Extended order, Close order and Arms drill; Anti-gas appliances drills etc	
"	19/6/17		Training:- 6 to 7.30 AM, 8.30 to 1 PM — same as for 18th.	
"	20/6/17		Training:- do for 19th.	
"	21/6/17		Training:- as " 20th.	
"	22/6/17		Training:- do " 21st.	
"	23/6/17		Training:- as " 22nd.	
"	24/6/17		Sunday. Church parades held	
"	25/6/17		Training:- under company arrangements.	
"	26/6/17		Training:- Musketry and Live Bomb Throwing at rifle range. Draft of 1 officer and 29 O Ranks joined Regt.	
"	27/6/17		Training:-	
"	28/6/17		Training:- 8-11 AM Lewis Gun Instr'n; Swedish drill; Close order and Arms drill. Extended order drill. 6-9 PM Battalion attack practice	

88

WAR DIARY

Army Form C. 2118.

1/5th South African Infy. Regt.

Place	Date	Hour	Summary of Events and Information	Remarks and references to Appendices
ARRAS	9/6/17		No change	
"Huts N Chain"	10/6/17		Battalion less working parties attached to XIII Corps Signals and 184th Coy (Tunnelling) R.E. moved to Y. Huttments by road.	
"	11/6/17		Draft of 29 other ranks joined Battn. from Base.	
"	12/6/17		10 Officers + 60 other ranks attached to 184th Tunn. Coy R.E. rejoined Battalion having been replaced by same number of 4th Regt.	
"	13/4/17		Training:- 6.30 to 7.30 a.m. Physical Training; 9-12 noon; Close order drill; rifle exercises and Lewis gun instruction.	
"	14/6/17		Training:- 6.30 - 7.30 A.M. Physical Training; 9-12 noon; Arms drill, Musketry, Bombing and Lewis Gun Instruction. 2-3 p.m. Army will fire practice.	
"	15/6/17		Training:- 6.30 - 7.30 a.m. Physical Training; 9 - 11 a.m. Lewis Gun Instruction, Bayonet fighting. 4.45 - 7.30 p.m. Sham attack operation on Coys training ground.	
"	16/6/17		Sham Operations against attached Battalions.	
"	17/6/17		Working parties required nines from Arras	

1577 Wt. W10791/1873 500,000 1/15 D.D.&L. A.D.S.S./Forms/C. 2118.

Army Form C. 2118.

WAR DIARY

or ~~Intelligence Summary~~ 1st South African Infantry

(Erase heading not required.)

Place	Date	Hour	Summary of Events and Information	Remarks and references to Appendices
ARRAS	1/6/17		Battalion - less A+D Coys - moved to ARRAS, travelling by train from AGNY-ST-FLOCHEL.	
	2/6/17		No change.	
	3/6/17		Working party of 5 Officers and 80 other ranks despatched to DINGWALL CAMP [ST LAURENT BLANGY] for night work under Capt Synnale.	VIII
	4/6/17		No change.	
	5/6/17		Working party at DINGWALL CAMP and 1 platoon from details in ARRAS merged into two composite battalions formed by S.A. Brigade moved up (6a)m as Divisional Reserve to attack carried out by 27th Infy Brigade. ar 8 p.m.	
	6/6/17		Working party returned to DINGWALL CAMP and platoon to ARRAS 6 p.m.	
	7/6/17		No change.	
	8/6/17		No change.	

40

WAR DIARY

Army Form C. 2118.

1st South African Infantry

WA/16

Place	Date	Hour	Summary of Events and Information	Remarks and references to Appendices
L'hute	1/1/17	—	Inspection. Church Services.	
	2/1/17	—	Training:— Close Order drill; Bayonet fighting; Dummy bombing; Patrol Reports; Musketry; Platoon attack practice, pitching Rifle Grenades; Physical and Recreational, Semaphore, Gun Instruction; Signalling, and Scouting and Sniping.	
	3/1/17	—	Training.	
	4/1/17	—	Training. 6-7am to 7.30 AM; 8-30 — 1 PM.	
	5/1/17	—	Training:— Firing at Range.	
	6/1/17	—	Battalion moved to SIMENCOURT.	
SIMENCOURT	7/1/17	—	Training. 6-7.30am; 8.30 — 1 PM.	
"	8/1/17	—	Sunday Church parade cancelled owing to inclement weather.	
"	9/1/17	—	Training:— 8 AM to 3 PM. at training area.	
"	10/1/17	—	Training:— Firing for all NCOs and men in the Battalion at Rifle Range.	
"	11/1/17	—	Training:— 8.30 — 10 AM. Coy Drill. 10 — 11.30. Bayonet Drill. 11.30 — 1 PM. Coy training.	

WAR DIARY

Army Form C. 2118.

Place	Date	Hour	Summary of Events and Information	Remarks and references to Appendices
Simencourt	22/7/17		Sunday. Church Parade – C. of E. Presbyterian, Wesleyan, Dutch Reformed and Roman Catholic.	
"	23-7-17		Training – 8.30 to Noon – musketry & Coy. training.	
"	24-7-17		Training – 9.30 to 11.30 A.m. Night operations. Bathing. Scheme. Coys. move off at 9 p.m.	
"	25-7-17		Training – 8 to 11 a.m. Route march under Coy. arrangements. Draft of 31 arrived.	
"	26-7-17		Training – No training – cleaning up of billets. Parade grounds etc.	
"	27-7-17		Entrained BEAUMETZ at 2.20 A.m. and proceeded to BAPAUME. arrived 5 A.m. by broad gauge. Left BAPAUME 5.30 Am by light railway and arrived RUYAULCOURT 11 Am.	
Ruyaulcourt	28.7.17		Marched from Ruyaulcourt for trenches (TRESCAULT) and relieved 2/5th. Batln. City of London Regt. Day very warm. Batln. on right carried out small raid during night. No identifications obtained – 1 Casualty – moving relieved believed killed.	

42

WAR DIARY

Army Form C. 2118.

Place	Date	Hour	Summary of Events and Information	Remarks and references to Appendices
Front line TRESCAULT	29/7/17		Several "whizz bangs" on front line & Sh for Riflegro started on space behind Battⁿ H.Q. Heavy rains and kailsorm. Trenches in very bad condition.	
"	30/7/17		A number of H.E. shells fell on front line 10 a.m. No damage done. Several H.E. shells fell on neighbourhood of Battⁿ H.Q. doing no damage 6 p.m. Night quiet. About 6 77 m.m. shells fired on DERBY & STAFFORD support between 6 and 9 a.m. Between 7 and 12 a.m. 5-4.2 shells fell at Junction of BASS LANE and Front line and five on No mans land. Enemy artillery quieter than on previous day. A large number of 4.2 shells fell along our front line and supports between 7 and 9 a.m. Seven 77 m.m. shells fell on STAFFORD SUPPORT at 10 a.m. Five 4.2 on STAFFORD SUPPORT at 9 p.m.	
"	31/7/17		At 11 p.m. a large patrol (1 officer and 30 O.R.) Proceeded into No MANS LAND to investigate hollow in ground. No sign of occupation found. A few burned out buildings were found. Probably an Estaminet	43

Army Form C. 2118.

WAR DIARY (2)

INTELLIGENCE SUMMARY. 1st South Af. Infy.

(Erase heading not required.)

Place	Date	Hour	Summary of Events and Information	Remarks and references to Appendices
Suverent	12/4/17	—	Training 6-7.30, 8.30 - 11 pm. Revolver Shooting.	
"	13/4/17	—	Training as for Summers and Officers.	
"	14/4/17	—	Training as for D.R.	
"	15/4/17	—	Sunday Church Parades.	
"	16/4/17	—	Training - Battn Scheme. 7.30 - 12.30 pm. At WALLY. Draft Capt. Style and 82 O.R. arrived. Training - Coy. Training 6-30 - 7.30 am Fring - Battn Competition - 8.30 am to 1 pm and 2-5 pm	
"	17/4/17	—	Training as for 16th.	
"	18/4/17	—	Brigade attack scheme at WALLY 7am to 3.30 Am.	
"	19/4/17	—	8 to 10 am Coy training 10 to 11 Battn drill. 2 to 5 Am Inter Platoon Marching Competition. Draft of sixteen arrived.	
"	—	—	Battalion Scheme as on 15/4/17. Move off at 8am.	44
"	20/4/17	—	Training 8.30 to 10 am Coy training. 11 to 11 am. Battn drill. 11.10 to 11 am. HQ. Transport and L. Gunners musketry competition. Final football match between 1st and 2nd Regts for Perkins Cup. Result 18-8 in favour 1st Regt.	
"	21/4/17	—	8.30 to 1 pm HQ. Transport and L. Gunners musketry competition. Final football match between 1st and 2nd Regts for Perkins Cup. Result 18-8 in favour 1st Regt.	

Army Form C. 2118

WAR DIARY
or
INTELLIGENCE SUMMARY
(Erase heading not required.)

Instructions regarding War Diaries and Intelligence Summaries are contained in F.S. Regs., Part II. and the Staff Manual respectively. Title Pages will be prepared in manuscript.

Place	Date	Hour	Summary of Events and Information	Remarks and references to Appendices
Trenches TRESCAULT	1/8/17		A Patrol consisting of one officer and one platoon left Bay 23 and proceeded to N.W. Corner BOAR COPSE, thence forward in No Man's Land. The enemy was not encountered and party returned at 1.55 a.m. Day very quiet.	
	2/8/17		Day very quiet.	

Jnkel
Lieut-Col
Comdg 1st S.A. Inf

46

FREZENBERG

EDITION 3.

1:10,000 Trenches Corrected From Information Received up to 21/8/17

Scale 1:10,000

WAR DIARY
or
INTELLIGENCE SUMMARY
(Erase heading not required.)

Army Form C. 2118

Instructions regarding War Diaries and Intelligence Summaries are contained in F. S. Regs., Part II. and the Staff Manual respectively. Title Pages will be prepared in manuscript.

Place	Date	Hour	Summary of Events and Information	Remarks and references to Appendices
METZ-EN-COUTURE	3/8/17		Battalion was relieved out of the line by the 3rd S. Infty and moved into Brigade Reserve.	
"	4/8/17		Working party for work in trenches supplied by 3 companies.	
"	5/8/17		-do-	
"	6/8/17		-do-	
"	7/8/17		-do-	
"	8/8/17		-do-	
"	9/8/17		Battalion took over the line in relief of 3rd S. Infty.	
TRENCHES [TRESCAULT SECTION]	10/8/17		Our artillery active during night shelling roads. 2 Officers and 20 O.Ranks patrolled, no mans land. 11-12 mm. Enemy artillery quiet - 1 O.Rank wounded.	
"	11/8/17		Our artillery active during night. Our patrol heavily fired on by M.Gs. Enemy artillery quiet. 1 O.Rank wounded.	
"	12/8/17		Our artillery active during the day. Patrol out during night	

WAR DIARY
or
INTELLIGENCE SUMMARY

(Erase heading not required.)

Army Form C. 2118

Instructions regarding War Diaries and Intelligence Summaries are contained in F. S. Regs., Part II. and the Staff Manual respectively. Title Pages will be prepared in manuscript.

Place	Date	Hour	Summary of Events and Information	Remarks and references to Appendices
YPRES	13/8/17		Our artillery active during the night. Enemy shelled the support line during the day. No damage.	
"	14/8/17		Our artillery fairly active. Usual patrol out during the night. Enemy artillery quiet. Six enemy observation balloons were up during the day.	
"	15/8/17		Usual patrol out. No enemy seen. Hostile aeroplanes patrolled our lines at 1.30pm	
"	16/8/17		Our artillery very active. Enemy artillery quiet.	
"	17/8/17		Battalion relieved out of line by 2nd Regt S.A. Infy.	
"	18/8/17		Day spent in cleaning up.	
"	19/8/17		Six Platoons provided as working parties. Remainder at Church parade.	
"	20/8/17		Training:- Physical training, Squad drill, Platoon provided to work on trenches.- Remainder.	
"	21/8/17		Platoon provided to work on trenches. Physical training, Arms Drill, Platoon and Company drill, Bayonet fighting, Musketry. Recreational Battn. drill. Remainder as for 21st.	
"	22/8/17		3 Platoons for working parties. Remainder as for 21st.	

Place	Date	Hour	Summary of Events and Information	Remarks and references to Appendices
YPRES	23/8/17		Five platoons provided for work. Remainder employed at training.	
"	24/8/17		Four platoons provided for work. Four more platoons were witnessed by the Corps a demonstration which were Divisional Commanders. Swam Aquatic Sports and Divisional Commanders were held during the afternoon.	
"	25/8/17		The Battalion and 1st Line transport inspected by Corps Commander.	
"	26/8/17		Sunday – Church Parades.	
"	27/8/17		Company training.	
ACHIET-LE-PETIT	28/8/17		Battalion moved to new area.	
"	29/8/17		Wet day. Company training.	
"	30/8/17		Training. Cleaning up. Reorganization of Platoons & Coys.	
"	31/8/17		Training. Drill. Battn Parade. Rifle Exercises, Bayonet training, Musketry Saluting, Inspection of Arms & gas appliances, Section and Platoon Drill.	

P. .... Major
LIEUT. COLONEL
COMMANDING 1st S.A. INFANTRY.

WAR DIARY or INTELLIGENCE SUMMARY

1st Bn. Queen's Regt.

Vol 18

Place	Date	Hour	Summary of Events and Information	Remarks and references to Appendices
ACHIET-LE-PETIT.	1/9/17		Training under Company arrangements. One Company firing at Range.	
"	2/9/17		Sunday - Church Parades.	
"	3/9/17		Training - Battalion drill, Bayonet fighting, Section, Platoon and Company training on range. Musketry. A Brigade Guard Mounting Competition was held during the afternoon with the following result:-	
			1st - Sgt Smith, 2nd Regt.	
			2nd - SA LTM Battery	
			3rd - Sgt Sayers, 2nd Regt.	
			4th - Sgt Sayers, 1st Regt.	
			5th - "B" Coy.	
"	4/9/17		The Battalion marched to the Butte de Warlencourt to visit the scene of the operations in which the Battalion took part on 16/20 October 1916.	
"	5/9/17		Training - Battalion drill 9 - 9.30. Marched to training ground and Companies practised Platoon & trench attack and Company attack.	

WAR DIARY or INTELLIGENCE SUMMARY

1st South African Infy.

Army Form C. 2118

Place	Date	Hour	Summary of Events and Information	Remarks and references to Appendices
AQUIET-LE-PETIT	4/9/17		Training:- Physical training, bayonet fighting, Bombing. Company drill, Musketry. Company in attack. Recreational.	
"	7/9/17		Training 8.30 to 12.30 pm Field firing. Battalion Sports in afternoon.	
"	8/9/17		Training 9.30 to 12.30 pm - Battalion attack practice.	
"	9/9/17		Sunday - Church parade.	
"	10/9/17 11/9/17		Training 8.30 to 12.30 pm -do-	
"	12/9/17		Battalion moved by march route and train to new area.	
WATOU	13/9/17		No change	
"	14/9/17		Battalion moved to Brandhoek billeting area.	
BRAND-HOEK	14/9/17		Coy at disposal of Coy Commanders	
"	15/9/17		Coy. at disposal of Coy Commrs	
"	16/9/17			
YPRES [FRESENBEEK Sector]	17/9/17		Battalion moved into support line in relief of 5 Lancs Fus.	

WAR DIARY No 3
INTELLIGENCE SUMMARY — 1st South African Infy.

Army Form C. 2118.

Place	Date	Hour	Summary of Events and Information	Remarks and references to Appendices
YPRES [FRIEZENBERG SECTOR]	18/9/17		See attached re. Offensive Operations.	
	19/9/17			
	20/9/17			
	21/9/17			
	22/9/17			
TORONTO CAMP	23/9/17		Battalion relieved from Reserve and moved by road to Toronto Camp.	
WINNIZEELE	24/9/17		Battalion moved by bus to Winnizeele area.	
—do—	25/9/17		Day spent in cleaning up and reorganization.	
—do—	26/9/17		No change.	
ARNEKE	27/9/17		Battalion moved by march all route to ARNEKE area	
—do—	28/9/17		training under Corps arrangement.	
—do—	29/9/17		training	
—do—	30/9/17		Sunday — Church Services.	

1/10/17

Dunedor
Major
Comdg. 1st Regt. S.A. Infy.

1st Regt. South African Infantry,
25/9/17.

SOUTH AFRICAN BRIGADE.

REPORT ON OPERATIONS 20/21st Sept., 1917.
S.W. OF ZONNEBEKE.

Ref. Map. FREZENBERG 1/10,000. Edn.3.

ASSEMBLY. The Battalion left their preparatory positions in vicinity of CAMBRIDGE ROAD at 11-30 pm. on night 19/20th September. Heavy rain had fallen rendering the going difficult and exceedingly treacherous.
    We moved to our assembly position, which had been taped earlier that evening in rear of 3rd Regiment, in single file in following order:- "A", "B", "D" and "C" Companies, "A", "B" and "D" Companies in order named from Right to Left in the leading line with "C" Company about 50 yards in their rear as support.
    Battalion HQrs. moved up at 12 midnight to 3rd Regt. HQrs. in a "pill box" at D.25.d.25.60.
    Assembly was completed by 3-30 am, but owing to a Company runner going astray I was unable to report completion until 5-10 am. Casualties during assembly were practically nil.

ADVANCE.   At ZERO 3rd Regiment moved forward to the attack, followed by the 1st Regiment about 100 yards in rear. Almost immediately the enemy's barrage came down and in consequence my leading line reduced their distance to 50 yards in rear of 3rd Regiment.
    The O/C.3rd Regiment moved forward at ZERO with his support Company and I remained at D.25.d.25.60 until 6-10 am when my attention was drawn by Captains DAVIES, 1st Regt., STOKES, 3rd Regt., and the O/C Coy., 5th Cameron Highlanders, in Brigade Reserve, to a number of men retiring on our right flank. I immediately pushed forward to about D.26.a.1.2 and found Captain SPRENGER, 3rd Regt., in charge at this point. The ground here was being swept by heavy M.G. fire from POTSDAM and our casualties were exceedingly heavy. Capt. SPRENGER told me he was held up from POTSDAM and I advised him that men of Brigade on our right had apparently fallen back. I instructed him to form a defensive flank with all available men of 1st and 3rd S.A.I. and endeavour to surround and capture the position. He fully appreciated the situation and the attack was immediately started led by Capt. SPRENGER and preceded by a Rifle Grenade Barrage, his party working from shell hole to shell hole round to the S. and the other party moving E. under Sergt. NICHOLLS, 1st Regt.
    The following is the report of work done by this party handed in by L/Cpl EATON, 1st Regt:-
    "As commanded I am herewith reporting the facts
    known to me concerning the taking of three "pill
    boxes at POTSDAM. As we reached them Sergt.
    NICHOLLS of "A" Coy., 1st Regt, dashed up to the
    entrance of the first "pill box" and at the point
    of the bayonet forced the garrison to surrender,
    doing the same to the next two. Sergt. NICHOLLS
    showed splendid dash and courage as the only
    support he had were my section, six all told.
    Between 20 and 30 prisoners were taken."
    I then pushed on to VAMPIRE to get touch with Col. Thackeray but failed to find him. The advance of the 1st Regiment appears to have been excellently carried
                                                        out ..

-2-.

out from ZERO onwards. The men were well in hand and did their work well.

On my left flank ("D" Coy) touch was maintained throughout with 2nd Regiment and no obstacles were encountered.

The Centre Company ("B") was responsible for maintaining direction, and the FREZENBERG-ZONNEBEKE ROAD was used.

The Right Company ("A") had heavy work and were unable to maintain touch with the Battalion on our right. I had detailed two sections and 2/Lieut. LAWRENCE to work beyond our Battalion Boundary and keep touch at all costs. I quote this Officer's report:-

"I pushed forward without serious opposition until I got in front of what apparently was POTSDAM. Here the section I was with came under very heavy machine gun fire. I got the men to advance from shell hole to shell hole. After having several casualties I halted to reconnoitre. I found I was well in front of the 3rd Regt. and, also that the troops on my right were falling back, leaving me with no support on my right. I collected all the men round about me and worked off to the right until I got to some derelict tanks. From there I worked up on the left bank of the railway. Here I found one Royal Scot and several of the 1st Regiment who were bombing a dugout on the right of the embankment. I gave them assistance. After a few minutes a German came out and surrendered, followed by twenty others. I sent them back to the rear. Here three machine guns were taken. One I noticed had been in action for some time. I sent a man to mark the guns as being captured by us. I know for certain of one gun being marked "1st S.A.I." I pushed on from there on the right of the embankment and chased out several of the enemy all along the line, most were shot, others made off too quickly. I was near the 1st objective before I noticed that the Royal Scots were hanging back about three hundred yards in front of the German front line. I went back and tried to get them to go forward. After some time they followed on. I then left them, crossed over the line and worked along the left of the embankment until I reached the final objective."

On reaching 1st objective I gave instructions regarding the reorganization and second advance and ascertained that all four Company Commanders were casualties.

Almost immediately on my arrival at 1st objective I saw some men of both regiments move through the barrage and attack enemy strong point at D.26.a.80.45 (Dressing Station). The party from 1st Regiment was headed by Sergt. FROHBUS. I followed them and on calling on the enemy to surrender, 2 Officers and between 30 and 40 men,(all Medical Corps) came out and were sent back as prisoners. The remainder refused to surrender. I ordered some men to blow in one of the loop holes, which they succeeded in doing, I believe with Mills' Hand Grenades, when a "P" bomb was thrown in. In a couple of minutes the whole place was in a sheet of flame with huge clouds of smoke issuing. I then formed up two parties on N. and S. corners of E. end of the stronghold, and had the enemy shot down as he bolted. I estimate 40 enemy machine gunners were shot here. There are 25 dead bodies in and about the entrance and 3 half burnt bodies inside the building. Besides these there is a string of dead trailing towards the enemy lines. No prisoners were taken. The fort yielded 4 M.G.

M.Gs.(3 heavy 1 light).

In the meantime some enemy were located in a small hedge about 50 yards to the N. of the fort. These were dealt with by 2/Lt.VINCENT and a Lewis Gun.

The advance for 2nd objective commenced at 7 am. Of the party who passed through our protective barrage to attack the strong point mentioned above, I am only able to record the death of 2 men from the Shrapnel barrage that passed over them.

The advance to 2nd Objective was uneventful and I was able to report at 7-50 am that the final objective had been taken and consolidation was proceeding with touch on both flanks.

CONSOLIDATION. The line chosen was about 100 to 150 yards on reverse side of the crest with outpost line on the crest to command the valley running parallel to and S.W. of the JACOBS HOUSE-STATION ROAD in D.21Central. This road was the line taken up by the enemy in his retreat. My dispositions were 3 Companies in front line and 1 Company about 100 yards in rear in support. Shell holes were connected up rapidly, care being taken to show distinct line as a mark for enemy fire, nor were sandbags used, except where necessary, and these were carefully camouflaged. Rifles were cleaned and tested, S.A.A. replenished, etc.

At about 4 pm in response to my request one Company of the 5th Cameron Highlanders was sent to reinforce and they were distributed and ordered to dig in along the line BREMEN REDOUBT-CONCRETE RAILWAY BRIDGE.

ENEMY COUNTER ATTACKS. The enemy made three attempts to counter attack on the 20th. The first attempt being the only really serious affair.

① At 10 am enemy started dribbling men in small parties over ridge D.21 Central into valley below with obvious intention of counter attacking from vicinity of BOSTIN FARM. At 10-15 am I wired this information and our barrage rapidly closed down causing enormous casualties in their ranks and completely smashed up the attempt. In the meantime heavy rifle, L.G. and M.G. fire was opened on the ridge at a range of 1,000 yards.

② At 10-50 am enemy were seen moving small parties S.W. along the ridge towards railway with intention of attacking from my right flank. This information was sent to Royal Scots. Our barrage again caught them together with rifle and M.G. fire. This was not by any means a serious attempt and it was obvious that he was losing heart. At 1 pm. I reported complete failure of counter attacks under our barrage and position satisfactory.

③ At 1-30 pm a third attempt was made in a half-hearted fashion to dribble men over ridge D.21 central into valley for counter attack. This was easily repulsed by vigorous rifle and M.G. fire and artillery.

At 10-55 am on 21st instant I wired that enemy were moving forward in small parties from buildings D.21.d.2.7 towards ZONNEBEKE CATHEDRAL. The F.O.O. was on the spot and artillery were rapidly brought to bear on this point.

At about 5-30 pm on 21st instant enemy laid down heavy barrage on our position with 5-9s and heavier guns. At 5-45 pm I was out of touch with my front line owing to the barrage and our M.Gs. opened on my left flank. I had been informed by C.R.A. that our combing barrage would open at 6 pm and decided to anticipate events so fired S.O.S. No attempt was however being made against my section. I have since learned that we were subjected to the heavy fire of enemy heavies while an attempt was being made by them to recapture Hill 37 some distance on our left flank. This heavy holding barrage was by far the heaviest bombardment we have been subjected to and lasted fully three hours.

OUR BARRAGE.
Was excellent throughout. During the advance it was easy to follow owing to the proportion of smoke shell used and I do not think our casualties from our own shells was out of proportion. There is no doubt in my mind that H.E. is the most deadly and effective barrage we have. I regard shrapnel as most ineffective by comparison. I have only to quote the case mentioned where our shrapnel passed over us with only two casualties.

H.E. has a most stimulating effect on our troops, who have every confidence in it, while I feel sure it is regarded by the enemy with the greatest fear and causes considerable demoralization. It is sufficient to point out that the terrain conditions were against H.E. on this occasion, viz., soft wet and shell hole pitted earth. Last, but not least wounds from H.E. incapacitate men immediately and are ghastly in the extreme.

I regret to have to record that during the advance one of our heavies was firing short the whole time and we suffered a number of casualties on our right flank in consequence. Also at 5-45 pm on the 21st the guns covering my right flank just N. of the railway blew in my front line and compelled me to withdraw all men from this point for the time being, besides causing several casualties. This is the more inexplicable as the placing had been perfect up to that time. I wired this at 5-50 pm and "pigeoned" it at 5-44 pm. The combing barrage laid down at 6 am on 21st was excellently timed and most effective. Any proposed attempt on the part of the enemy to spring a counter attack on us at dawn would have been completely defeated.

ENEMY BARRAGE.
This has been dealt with in the narrative. Beyond the barrage laid down at ZERO on our front line and the holding barrage of heavies on afternoon and evening of 21st their shelling was intermittent and ineffective.

M.G. BARRAGE.
I saw no effects of this barrage, nor was I at any time able to follow it owing to the din of the artillery.

RELIEF.
Was completed during night of 21st/22nd without serious incident. It is curious that my last Coy. did not get clear until about 7 am on 22nd and my only gas cases occurred to them on the way out, 4 men being slightly gassed by gas shell.

CARRIERS.
I would suggest that the number of Brigade Carriers be considerably increased and if possible equipped with more Yukon Packs which are far and away the best form of transport under these conditions.

SNIPING.
Considerable sniping with both rifle and M.G. at about 1,000 yards range was done by us. The enemy worried us considerably with M.G. fire from

from Hill 37 due N. of our line during both 20th and 21st, while a little individual sniping was done by his snipers as well.

CASUALTIES.

I suffered heavy casualties from hostile barrage soon after ZERO. The attacking waves were accordingly closed up to 50 yards distance from 3rd Regiment to clear this area and casualties ceased. This was in accordance with instructions issued prior to the advance.

Heavy casualties were caused later on by the concentrated enfilade M.G. fire from POTSDAM.

By midday 20th I had no stretchers or stretcher bearers left, the latter being casualties.

to C.C.S. — As far as I can gather, evacuation of wounded back was rapid, but the prisoners and stretcher bearers working in advance of R.A.P. failed to reach my line and in consequence stretcher cases who were hit before 8 am on the 20th were not cleared until the morning of the 21st.

It was impossible to evacuate stretcher cases during the hours of darkness.

Total Casualties:-	Offrs.	O/Ranks.
Killed	2	56
Wounded	7	250
Wounded - at duty	3	23
Missing		8
TOTAL.	12	337

GENERAL.

The fight was essentially a soldiers battle, full of individual acts of gallantry and marked throughout by the greatest dash. The "Bullet and Bayonet" spirit prevailed and from the start all were out to win at any cost. At only one period were matters critical, the capture of POTSDAM settled the question. The trouble throughout was to direct and restrain the keenness of fighting spirit displayed by all ranks.

I consider that the attack formation adopted the most suitable for this nature of warfare and properly handled with good well-trained men the "pill box" offers no serious obstacle to our advance and it most certainly proves a deathtrap to the enemy. The principle must however be borne in mind that on no account is the line to advance without wiping up everything in rear.

All the "pill boxes" I saw covered one another, and all fired to the rear or flank. This should enable our troops to tackle them without serious difficulties.

Bombs were practically not used but should be carried at the rate of one per man.

Rifle grenades are very effective on suspected shell holes and snipers.

Entrenching tools were left behind and spade only carried. This proved an excellent exchange.

It is most essential that the cult of the bullet and bayonet should be practised and every man have a knowledge of the Lewis Gun.

1st Regt. South African Infantry,
25/9/17.

SOUTH AFRICAN BRIGADE.

COMMUNICATION.

Copies of messages sent are attached.

I was extremely unfortunate to lose the greater proportion of my HQr. Signallers and Runners, together with the signalling equipment, lamps, etc., from the enemy barrage soon after zero. This proved a serious handicap.

At D.25.d.25.60 I established an advanced report centre under my Adjutant and Signalling Officer from zero onwards. At this station we had in use a Power Buzzer and Fullerphone to Brigade HQrs. and a telephone to the Royal Scots on our Right Flank. The Artillery F.O.O. also established his instrument here and was able to maintain communication throughout 20th instant. This kept me practically in direct touch with our Artillery and was of invaluable assistance.

From D.25.d.25.60 to my Battle HQrs. at D.26.a.80.45 communication was maintained by runner and on night of 20th by Lucas Lamp.

During afternoon of 20th my Adjutant and Signalling Officer joined me at Battle HQrs. and thereafter the station at D.25.d.25.60 was maintained by my Signalling Sergt.

On morning of 21st Artillery F.O.O. ran a line from D.25.d.25.60 and thence on to the front line. This line held until evening of 21st when heavy bombardment laid down by the enemy destroyed it.

PIGEONS.

One message only was sent by me - vide Appendix. The number of pigeons issued was so small that I felt that they should be retained for an emergency - hence did not use them more frequently. They are undoubtedly of the greatest value and the issue should be increased.

LUCAS LAMPS.

Were of the utmost value. _Every_ message sent by me was picked up at D.25.d.25.60. At night the ruby shade was used. Receipt of the message by day was notified by waving the arm.

RUNNERS.

My runners were most reliable and except for the casualties caused early in the operations I suffered few losses.

CONTACT AEROPLANE.

Flares were lit on arrival at our objective (2nd objective) when called for, and were, I believe, picked up by the Contact Aeroplane. Our Aeroplane signalling equipment was destroyed and we were unable to communicate with them by this means.

Messages despatched by 1st Regiment, South African
Infantry, during Operations of 20/22nd Sept. 1917.

20th 2-5 am. HQ. 1st with 3rd Regt.

4-50 am Three Companies in assembly positions. One not yet reported.

5-10 am Assembly completed.

7-50 am Second Objective taken. All going well. Casualties slight.

9-00 am Casualties heavy. Estimated rifles 300. Enemy barraging. Am digging in. In touch on flanks. Suggest reinforcements. Send S.A.A.

10-15 am Enemy advancing to counterattack in small parties. Send up S.A.A. Urgent.

10-45 am To Royal Scots. Enemy advancing to counter attack in small parties.

1-00 pm Counter attack failed under our heavy barrage. Enemy can be seen moving about in BOSTIN FARM. Situation satisfactory. S.O.S. Signals and S.A.A urgently needed. Not a single stretcher been up here yet. I have a number of cases waiting. Please expedite.

1-35 pm Counter attack massing D.26.b.8.6. Royal Scots have withdrawn to right of Railway. Send S.O.S. grenades.
  (The above message was repeated to G.O.C. 27th Brigade who was at HQrs. of Royal Scots).

2-10 pm Enemy are again advancing to the valley in front of my line. Some of Enemy are retiring. There is evidently a whizbang gun in house at D.21.a.60.45. S.A.A. arrived. Send S.O.S. signals.

2-30 pm. Send stretcher bearers.

4-00 pm Situation satisfactory. Intermittent enemy shelling, one Company reinforcements arrived. Now consolidating line Concrete Railway Arch to BREMEN REDOUBT. Dispositions three Companies S.A.I. in front line, one Company in support, one Company Camerons in reserve. Total rifles S.A.I. about 250. Spirits good.

21st 6-15 am Situation satisfactory. No stretcher bearers, rations or water yet arrived.

10-20 am Casualties up to 12 noon 21st. Killed 40 other ranks. Wounded. Major T.G.McEWEN, Captains J.T.BAIN, T.O.PRIDAY, K.KEITH. 2/Lieuts. B.H. O'CONNELL, H.T.W.BARKER, F.G.TYERS and 260 other ranks.

10-30 am Situation satisfactory. Enemy appear to be holding line JACOBS HOUSE, STATION, through D.21.central. BOSTIN FARM is apparently held by enemy. Enemy are dribbling small parties into valley D.21.c. Artillery should pay attention to this valley as probably dumping off

2.

off place for counter attacks.   Continual movement JACOBS HOUSE and LEVI COTTAGES. F.O.O. is with me here.   Plentifully supplied with S.A.A. and rations. All wounded now clear.

10-55 am. Enemy seen moving in small parties from buildings at D.21.d.2.7 towards ZONNEBEKE CATHEDRAL. Parties of enemy also seen moving around JACOBS HOUSE carrying red cross flags.

1-15 pm. Situation satisfactory. Enemy machine gun actively sniping from apparently HILL 37. Our snipers active on enemy about JACOBS AND LEVI HOUSE.

8-25 pm. Your BM.907 and DL.7 received. No attack on my front. Shelling very heavy and my HQ. receiving particular attention with at least 5.9; probably heavier.

22nd 9-35 am. Relief complete.

The following pigeon message was despatched at 5-44 pm on 21/9/17.

"Our barrage shelling my right flank. Can this be stopped.

5.50 P.M. *Our artillery have almost blown our line away on the right near railway.*

COPY.

1ST SOUTH AFRICAN INFANTRY BRIGADE.

1st REGIMENT.

Please send to this office not later than 8 am tomorrow, answers to the following queries. An extra copy is sent in order that the reply might be written against the question. This information is required by Division.

CARRYING PARTIES.

(a) How detailed .... By Coys.
(b) Strength .... 2 Sections per Coys.
(c) What carried .... S.A.A. Very Lights. S.O.S. Signals L.G.Magazines (Spare).
(d) If successful .... Yes.

TRENCH MORTARS.

(a) How employed. ....)
(b) Ammunition carried etc.) No.

RIFLE GRENADES.

Cases where used and what results ... (1) by 3rd Regt. on POTS-dam. Result not known. (2) Against a sniper after 2nd objective was reached. (3) On suspected shell holes after 2nd objective was reached (2) and (3) were successful.

USE OF RIFLES.

Were they used in dealing with strong points, etc. .... Used to wipe out enemy after they bolted from their strong point.

PACE OF BARRAGE.

Was it suitable. .... Too slow under the dry conditions prevailing during part of advance.

HOSTILE BARRAGE.

(a) History of it. .... Laid down very rapidly and heavily
(b) When it came down...... on our front line after ZERO,
(c) When it was heaviest .. causing me heavy casualties. We were then free of it until enemy aeroplanes had located extent of our advance when they barraged our new line. Heavy barrage of 5.9s and larger guns laid on us at 5-45 pm on 21st.

MOPPING UP.

(a) History of. .... No "Moppers Up" were detailed. This
(b) How detailed. .... work was done by sections from front line on the principle that no point was to be left unguarded.

USE OF RIFLE GRENADES AND MILLS HAND GRENADES.

(a) How many carried by
   (1) Battalions ...... R.G. 64 Rifle Grenadiers at 15 per man = 960.
                                    H.G. 1 per man = 500 approx.
   (2) Brigades.

(2).

(b) How carried in case of rifle grenades. ...... Some Coys. carried them stuck in their belts, others used a canvas carrier.

NORMAL ATTACK FORMATION.
   (a) Were they adhered to, and were they satisfactory. .. Attack formation as practised prior to operations was adhered to, and proved most successful.

   (b) If not what changes were made.

ANY FIRING FROM THE HIP. ...... Little if any.

WAS S.O.S. RIFLE GRENADE SATISFACTORY. Yes.

FORMING OF DEFENSIVE FLANK. .... Formed at 6-30 am on 20th
   Description of any case of. by 1st and 3rd Regts. under Captain SPRENGER, against POTSDAM.

WATER BOTTLES.
   Any extra water carried ...... No. Water was not received beyond water bottles carried until 21st.

WAS ISSUE OF MAPS, PLANS, OBLIQUES, ETC. SATISFACTORY. Yes.

HOSTILE COUNTER ATTACKS. .... 10 am 20th. Enemy seen dribbling in small parties from ridge in D.21 central towards hollow in vicinity of BOSTIN FARM. Dispersed by our artillery and rifle fire 10-50 am. Enemy seen moving in small parties along ridge towards railway as if to attack from right flank. Nothing further developed. Our snipers were very busy during this time.
1-30 pm. Enemy again advancing in small numbers from D.21 central towards valley. Dispersed by vigorous sniping and artillery fire.

ANY HOSTILE MACHINE GUN FIRE FROM BEHIND.
                        Yes. From POTSDAM in our right rear until this strong point was captured.

                        Sd. F.H.Heal,
                              Lt-Col,
25/9/17   Comdg. 1st Regt. S.A.Infy.

Army Form C. 2118.

WAR DIARY
or
INTELLIGENCE SUMMARY.
(Erase heading not required.)

1st South African Infantry

Instructions regarding War Diaries and Intelligence Summaries are contained in F.S. Regs., Part II and the Staff Manual respectively. Title pages will be prepared in manuscript.

Place	Date	Hour	Summary of Events and Information	Remarks and references to Appendices
ARNEKE AREA	1/10/17		Training under Company arrangements – 9-12 noon. Classes 2 to 3 pm and Recreational during afternoon.	
"	2/10/17		As for 1st.	
"	3/10/17		Training under Coy arrangements	
"	4/10/17		Battalion moved to Moulle by road	
MOULLE	5/10/17		Coy training on training ground.	
"	6/10/17		Training under Coy arrangements.	
"	7/10/17		Musketry :- Battalion firing at range.	
"	8/10/17		Battalion attack practice at the training ground.	
"	9/10/17		Coy Platoon and Section drill. Firing at range from 3 to 5:30 pm.	
BRAKE CAMP REIGERSBG	10/10/17		Battalion moved by tram to BRAKE CAMP " " march route to REIGERSBURG – details not for the line marches to HOUTTERQUE	77
CANAL BANK YPRES	11/10/17		Moved to CANAL BANK – Casualties in trekking parties 3 Officers wounded 8Ranks 2 killed 17 wounded 1 Off. and 2 ORanks gassed	63

WAR DIARY 1st South African Infy

INTELLIGENCE SUMMARY

Place	Date	Hour	Summary of Events and Information	Remarks and references to Appendices
YPRES CHEDDAR VILLA	13/10/17		Battalion moved up to Support line. Casualties 3 O/Ranks wounded	
	14/10/17		Casualties 2 Killed and 3 O/Ranks wounded.	
	15/10/17		Weather bad. Hostile artillery active during 24 hours	
	16/10/17		Our artillery active on PASHENDALE RIDGE. Hostile artillery fired HV shells in vicinity, Cemetery, BURNS HOUSE and Duckboard track to WINCHESTER FARM Casualties Hostile Infantry quiet.	
Front Line	17/10/17		Our artillery active on RIDGE. Hostile active whilst during 24 hours firing on BURNS HOUSE, SHAFT, OXFORD HOUSE, and duckboard track. Heavy barrage put on our front line at 9-30 A.M. Relieved 4th Regt. S.A. Infy on front line 16/17th. Casualties 2 Killed + Died of wounds 22 wounded.	
	18/10/17		Our artillery quiet during the day, but became active in the night. Hostile artillery very active during morning. Enemy aircraft also active. Casualties 1 O/Rk Killed 6 wounded.	

WAR DIARY
or
INTELLIGENCE SUMMARY 1st South African Infantry
(Erase heading not required.)

Place	Date	Hour	Summary of Events and Information	Remarks and references to Appendices
ST-POL-SUR-MER	28/10/17		Sunday – Church parade.	
OOST DUNKIRK BAINS	29/10/17		Moved by lorries to OOSTDUNKIRKBAINS and relieved 12th E. Surrey Regt in Right Section COXYDE BAINS Coast Defence Sector. Two Companies in occupation of posts and two Companies in Reserve.	
"	30/10/17		Quiet day. A few shells fired into OOSTDUNKIRK BAINS. Working parties.	
"	31/10/17		Quiet. Enemy fired a few H.V. shells in neighbourhood of OOST DUNKIRK BAINS between 7 and 9 p.m. Working parties provided.	

F.M.K.
LIEUT. COLONEL.
COMMANDING 1st S.A. INFANTRY.

WAR DIARY or INTELLIGENCE SUMMARY

Army Form C. 2118

1st South African Infantry

Place	Date	Hour	Summary of Events and Information	Remarks and references to Appendices
Front Line HÜBNER.	19/10/17		Own artillery very active on PASCHENDAELE RIDGE. Enemy artillery active. Casualties 3 other ranks missing.	
(incl. BURNS)	20/10/17		Own artillery quiet. Hostile artillery active, especially on BURNS HOUSE and dicklerud tracks. Relieved after dark out of front line, and moved to canal Bank.	
"	21/10/17		Day spent in cleaning clothing etc.	
"	22/10/17		Working party 4 off[ice]rs and 250 Rank & File supplied to digging cable trench. Casualties 1 killed, 1 wounded.	
NOUVEAU MONDE	23/10/17		Moved by bus to NOUVEAU MONDE.	
WORMHOUT	24/10/17		Battalion marched to WORMHOUT. Details reported from Houlergue.	
S[ain]t POL-SUR-MER McDURKAR(?)	25/10/17		Moved to SPL-SUR-MER.	
"	26/10/17		Day given to cleaning up.	
"	27/10/17		Companies at disposal of Company Commanders.	

WAR DIARY
or
INTELLIGENCE SUMMARY

1st South African Infy Vol 20

(Erase heading not required.)

Instructions regarding War Diaries and Intelligence Summaries are contained in F.S. Regs., Part II. and the Staff Manual respectively. Title Pages will be prepared in manuscript.

Place	Date	Hour	Summary of Events and Information	Remarks and references to Appendices
OOST DUNKIRK BAINS	1/11/17		Quiet. A few shells were fired into OOST DUNKERKE BAINS during the evening.	
"	2/11/17 Night		Quiet. Hostile Artillery slightly active. A small concentration (calibre unknown) was fired into OOST DUNKERKE BAINS between 9 and 9.15 pm	
"	3/11/17		Hostile artillery active. Several loads were dropped by Enemy aircraft at OOST DUNKIRK BAINS between 9 and 10 AM. No damage done.	
"	4/11/17		Hostile artillery active during the day.	
"	5/11/17		Hostile artillery fairly quiet.	
"	6/11/17		Enemy artillery active during afternoon.	
"	7/11/17		Quiet.	
"	8/11/17		... A few shells fired into Oost Dunkerke Bains at 2 am	
In front of Nieuwpoort Bains Section	9/11/17		Battalion relieved at 9 P.M. by 8th (S) Bn. Black Watch and moved to Yorkshire Camp. Left Yorkshire Camp at 10 p.m. and relieved the 7th Seaforth Hdrs. in the front line on the right Section Oost Dunkerque formation by 16 Gothas circled over Yorkshire Camp turning out searchlights on return — Anti-aircraft put five Lewis guns into action returning in South Easterly direction from bomb droppings.	67

WAR DIARY or INTELLIGENCE SUMMARY

Army Form C. 2118

Place	Date	Hour	Summary of Events and Information	Remarks and references to Appendices
In front line Macao-Post Bois sixteen	10/4/17		The Relief work affected without any casualties. A+B held the front trenches with D Coy in support. Our artillery shelled Lombaert 3yde from 2.15 to 2.45 pm. The Battalion H.Qrs was intermittently shelled by the enemy, who also shelled Rilles Suicide Corner with 5.9s. Between 7 pm & 1.30 a.m. East Dunkerque Road & back areas intermittently shelled by Enemy.	
	11/4/17		Our artillery intermittently shelled enemy lines in neighbourhood of Lombaert Zyde. From 7.25 a.m. to 7.30 a.m. three of our planes patrolled our front & were heavily shelled by enemy anti-aircraft. The enemy fired a number of Field-Howitzer into the right of our right Sub-Sector. Enemy fired what appeared to be small white balls these shot ups when our lines & on impact burst into a white cloud.	
	12/4/17		Our artillery heavily shelled neighbourhood of Lombaert 3yde. Our planes flew over the enemy lines at a low altitude. It was not fired at. At 6 a.m. the Enemy actively shelled East Dunkerque Rd with light H.E. & Shrapnel, and again at 9 p.m. Five Gas Shells fell near A Coy. Headquarters. Our back areas heavily shelled at intervals during the day. Enemy observed to be trying travelling kines along Canal. Considerable movement observed in enemy lines. Heavy clouds of smoke seen rising from direction of Lombaert Zyde	

INTELLIGENCE SUMMARY

(Erase heading not required.)

Place	Date	Hour	Summary of Events and Information	Remarks and references to Appendices
A front line Nieuport Bains section	13/XI/17		Bombardment by our artillery. From your fitness engaged & fired two rounds phos to retaliate. From your front & close support lines between 2.5 & 2.20 pm heavy fire near Boschl. Lane. One gas shell also fell in this sector at 11.30 p.m. One German was killed by our lower front line near a Pill Box. 12 Gothas accompanied by search-lights over lines, formation broken up by our anti-aircraft fire.	
	14/11/17		Our artillery very quiet all day. Between 1.40 & 2.50 p.m. enemy put 47 (4.2) shells on our machine gun positions in support lines near Bosche St. putting two m. guns and 1 pounder into action. At 3.30 pm another 20 (4.2) shells were put in the same position. Enemy trench mortars during the night on the left Baths sector. Two shells dropped on Beacon St. Five Gothas were seen at 6.15 am observing in the direction of Nieuport Bains.	
	15/11/17		Our artillery fired 22 heavy shells in vicinity of WESTENDE. From 3.15 to 3.50 p.m. five of our aeroplanes flew over the enemy lines. They were heavily shelled. Bullets resembling small very lights which burst into a cloud when starting the ground were also fired at them. Between 11.25 & 11.45 am the enemy fired 108 shells into our front & support lines between 1.5 & 2 pm. 146 shells fell in our line and 188 shells fell into support between 2.35 & 2.50 pm. 3.30 & 3.45 pm 81 shells also fell on our close support. Between 3.30 & 3.45 pm enemy observation planes flew continually over our lines from 6.30 to 11 am. At 2 pm enemy planes and lines into our trenches. One Photograph was obtained at 3.30 pm will look in the enemy lines.	

Place	Date	Hour	Summary of Events and Information	Remarks and references to Appendices
In front line Nieuport-Bains Section	16/10/17		Our artillery was less active than usual. The enemy at 10 p.m. fired a few shells on Coxt Dunkirk Road; & twenty (20) Dunlin Dunes was also shelled but the artillery was less active than usual. At 11 p.m. & 2 7 M.s fell on the right sub sector behind Road close support & at 11.15 p.m. ten (10) fell near enemy Hqrs night cab sector.	
"	17/10/17		Our field and heavy artillery fires between 10.30 p.m. & 11 p.m. 62 shells which exploded in vicinity of March House. The enemy fired thirty-six (36) shrapnel and H.E. shells in the vicinity of our support line. Four of his trench mortar shells fell in the rear down close support near Boche Lane. Only one enemy phone could was cut at 3.30 p.m. but returned immediately. The Battalion was relieved in the trenches by the 1st French 161st Infantry. The relief was effected without any casualties at 9.20 p.m. The Battalion arrived at Yorkshire at 12 midnight.	
YORKSHIRE CAMP	18/10/17		Quiet. One shell was fired into the camp at 3 a.m.	
LA PANNE	19/10/17		Battalion paraded to LA PANNE for march route at 2 p.m. on arriving there at 3.45 p.m.	
	20/10/17		Battalion marched to ALXEM	
	21/10/17		Battalion marched to WORMHOUDT	

WAR DIARY
INTELLIGENCE SUMMARY.

Army Form C. 2118.

Place	Date	Hour	Summary of Events and Information	Remarks and references to Appendices
	22/11		Battalion marched to WAEMAERS-CAPPEL	
	23/11		Battalion marched to HEURINGHEM	
	24/11		Battalion marched to WAVRANS	
	25/11		Battalion marched to ERGNY.	
ERGNY	26/11	A.M.	Reorganisation.	
"	27/11	8.30 to 12.30pm	Musketry training - Physical and Bayonet fighting	
		2pm to 4pm	Anti-gas drill, Platoon and Company drill - Afternoon Recreational	
"	28/11		Battalion parade and training as for 27/11/17.	
"	29/11		Training as for 28/11/17. Lubrication of breech etc to 266 Pte. W. R. SAUNDERS and 146 Pte. Goddard Q. Sup 6.0.	
"	30/11		Training as for 29/11/17.	

Signed
Lieut Colonel
Commanding 1st S.H. Inf. Regt.

WAR DIARY / INTELLIGENCE SUMMARY

Army Form C. 2118.

1 S A Sup/Bn
Vol 21

Place	Date	Hour	Summary of Events and Information	Remarks and references to Appendices
ERGNY.	1/12/17		2d Battalion marched to CREPY.	
	2/12/17		3d Battalion marched to ANVIN and entrained at 4.15 pm.	
	3/12/17		Detrained at PERONNE at 11 am and marched to YORK CAMP, MOISLAINES. One company employed as ort loading party to Brigade group from 10 am 3/12/14 to 9.30 pm 3/12/14. The Battalion marched to FNS. and from there proceeded to the line relieving 2/3 Batt IRISH GUARDS on the outpost line of the right sub-section of the GOUZECOURT sector — Gonnelieu	
GOUZECOURT	4/12/17		Nil. Our artillery was very active from 9.30 am to 10 pm. Our aircraft was not active. Two flights of fourteen machines passed over our line travelling N.E. Enemy artillery intermittently fired throughout the 24 hours mostly directed on Gouzecourt where a small ammunition dump was exploded at 3.15 pm. At 12 mn. 30 small shells fell just short of the night position of our outpost line.	

Place	Date	Hour	Summary of Events and Information	Remarks and references to Appendices
GOUZECOURT	5/2/17		One enemy aeroplane flew over our lines at 9 am and a pair came over at 11.30 am and returned flying low for some time. Our anti-aircraft guns opened up in each case. At 3 pm the 3rd Cav. Brigade reported that a number of enemy mtd men in VILLERS-GUISLAIN and report all but opened and continued until 4 pm. This turned out to be an enemy D.A.A. dump which had been blown up. Casualties – nil.	
–do–	6/2/17		Our artillery opened heavy fire at 6.5 am and continued for about half an hour. Flight of ten of our machines passed over the enemy line at 2.25 pm. Enemy artillery active throughout the day. Lewis machine guns active throughout the night. Casualties – wounded 3 ORs.	
–do–	7/2/17		Our artillery active. Large squadrons of our aeroplanes were continually crossing over the enemy's lines and enemy's Enemy artillery very active, dropping shells along our support line and on GOUZECOURT. Casualties: killed 2 ORs, wounded 2 ORs.	

Place	Date	Hour	Summary of Events and Information	Remarks
GOUZEAUCOURT	9.12.17		The Battalion relieved the 3rd S.W.B. in the front line at 9 a.m. The enemy shewed a heavy bombardment on our front line which lasted for an hour. Our snipers & Lewis gunners were very successful in sniping a few enemy snipers. Casualties were nil. No patrols were sent out.	
-do-	9.12.17		Our artillery was fairly active. Two patrols were sent out by the Company on the night. It was known that the enemy concentrated an average rifle & M.G. fire. Enemy artillery was active throughout the day. An enemy patrol was observed the enemy right of our sector and Lewis guns opened on it. In another sector M.G.s commanded a Co.	
-do-	10.12.17		Our artillery was fairly active. One of our aeroplanes engaged an enemy machine at 11.30 a.m. one of which was seen to come down. Patrols went out from the right company to our line. Nothing abnormal occurred during the night and remained in front of our line. Stops found our trenches. A patrol from the left company located the enemy 2760. at 4.30 p.m.	

Place	Date	Hour	Summary of Events and Information	Remarks and references to Appendices
GOUZEAUCOURT			brought in an I.M. that was out later went out with an R.E. party who destroyed the remaining 2 M.Gs. Up blowing them up. Enemy artillery fairly active. At 6 p.m. a heavy bombardment was opened up on vicinity of front line and at 10 p.m. a bombardment right close our front Company. Enemy aircraft were extremely flying over 10 and 10.30 a.m. a squadron of 20 machines. Between our lines in spite of our AA guns being no damage. A great deal of talking was heard from the enemy lines at dusk 3 men apart could be heard in the vicinity of	
VILLERS - GUISLAIN - Gonnelieu - wounded 2 O.Rs.			The Battalion was relieved by the 2nd Bn D.G. of and with draw to the support line. Our artillery was fairly active. Several of our aeroplanes flew over the enemy lines early in the morning. Enemy artillery was unusually quiet. At 4.30 a.m. relieved Bn was marched to its new billets in huts GOUZEAUCOURT	
	11 A.M.			

Army Form C. 2118.

WAR DIARY
or
INTELLIGENCE SUMMARY.
(Erase heading not required.)

76

Place	Date	Hour	Summary of Events and Information	Remarks and references to Appendices
GOUZEAUCOURT	12.12.17		The Regt. was relieved by the 3rd A.I. Infantry at midnight & returned to huts on the FINS-GOUZEAUCOURT Road. Our artillery was fairly active. Enemy artillery and M.G. were also active.	
HUTMENTS	13.12.17		The Battalion rested and received post, indent & damage.	
	14. P.M.		A few small shells fell in the camp doing no damage.	
GOUZECOURT	15.12.17		The Bn. relieved the 2nd 2nd Bn. in the front line. There certainly was not out support or our own bit neither did anything to prevent Enemy artillery was active particularly so from 3.30am to 6.30am. Thought it might be an attack but firing died out when to report on small parties of the enemy seen out support. At 1 am. two small parties of the enemy each were seen patrolling. Both were fired upon, one party got away. Two of the other ran into our wire and were captured. Signals from VILLERS-GUISLAIN and olaured during the night. Casualties nil. Enemy artillery quiet. Usual reports nothing to report. Our	

1577 Wt. W10791/1773 500,000 1/15 D.D.&L. A.D.S.S./Forms/C. 2118.

WAR DIARY or INTELLIGENCE SUMMARY

Place	Date	Hour	Summary of Events and Information	Remarks
GOUZEAUCOURT	6/4/17		Aircraft unusually active. Casualties nil.	
	7/4/17		A patrol left our line at 9 pm returning at 9.10 pm. No enemy was encountered. A patrol was out from 4.30am to 6.30am and had nothing to report. Enemy artillery was unusually quiet but shelling GONNELIEU during the night. Enemy traffic was heard in GONNELIEU during the night. Enemy plane flew over our line at 9am but was driven away by A.A. fire. Two patrols were sent out about our centre opposite the hay. Casualties nil. Two men wounded.	
-do-			3 patrols left our trenches from the right company, one from 5.30am to 6.30am, a second from 9.10pm and a third from 4.30pm to 6.30am. The first went along VILLIERS TRENCH to CEMETERY ROAD, saw ten armed about 30x and turned off and retired until they saw the flash of a shell close to our line when they went till along halted them, no they returned. The enemy put down small gun. The enemy halted them along the whole of the left front but had patrols out along the whole of the left front but had nothing to report. Our patrols went out from the left coy and had nothing to report. Would anything was.	

Army Form C. 2118.

WAR DIARY
or
INTELLIGENCE SUMMARY.
(Erase heading not required.)

Instructions regarding War Diaries and Intelligence Summaries are contained in F. S. Regs., Part II. and the Staff Manual respectively. Title pages will be prepared in manuscript.

Place	Date	Hour	Summary of Events and Information	Remarks and references to Appendices
GOUZEAUCOURT	19/2/19		Quiet night and obtained our relief late on front line. Our day patrols of about 15 rank were sent to watch the GONNELIEU-VILLERS GUISLAIN street at 9.30am. At 10.30pm our men parties of the 2nd and 3rd Lts went out along the front line. The enemy put up flares during the night of large calibre shells seen to burst on GONNELIEU at 3'o'clock am. Casualties nil.	
-do-	20/2/19		At 12.30am was relieved by the 2nd D.L. Inf. & proceeded to BRIGADE support. 4 of our shells fell within the vicinity of our front line & map reference... no hostile patrols were observed during our march. W. Casualties nil.	
-do-	21/2/19		No change. Casualty... R... unusual. An unusual shell was dropped on Gouzeaucourt and our left in front in line, was at 2.30 ...	
-do-	22/2/19		During the day the enemy shelled Gouzeaucourt our...	

WAR DIARY or INTELLIGENCE SUMMARY

Place	Date	Hour	Summary of Events and Information	Remarks and references to Appendices
Gouzeaucourt	20/2/17		2 enemy planes flew over at 8 a.m. Our A.A. guns fired up without result. Casualties NBC. 1 wounded. Enemy patrol left our trenches at 10 p.m. and moved east. 10 x what they kind sounded a distant musical instrument and singing. Two other patrols had nothing to report. Enemy artillery were active throughout the 24 hours. A large working party of from 200 to 300 men were seen, that went reported to the artillery who dispersed them. Enemy M.G. were very active, covering their working parties. Enemy planes were over our lines from 11 a.m. to 2 p.m.	
	21/2/17		Artillery fairly quiet. A few shells fell along support and front lines. Small enemy working parties seen behind front line.	
	22/2/17		Battalion was relieved by 2nd Regt. S.A.I. and became Regt in Reserve at hutments in W.C.3. Enemy shelled hutments causing two casualties.	

Army Form C. 2118.

WAR DIARY
or
INTELLIGENCE SUMMARY.
(Erase heading not required.)

Place	Date	Hour	Summary of Events and Information	Remarks and references to Appendices
Hermies Near 71NS	29/12/17		Men cleaning up, and undergoing foot treatment.	
	30/12/17		The Battalion was bathed at HEUDECOURT. Enemy shelled Hermies again, causing 12 casualties (1 killed and 11 wounded). Men forced to take refuge in Sunken road near Hermies. Enemy again shelled Hermies about 5 pm. Regt. moved into Sunken road. No casualties.	
	31/12/17	5 am.	Enemy fired a few gas shells and they shelled with medium calibre shells. No casualties. Preparations made to relieve 2nd S.A.I in line. At 30 pm. Regt. moved into line and relieved 2nd Regt. S.A.I. Relief carried out by 8 pm. No casualties.	

Jenkal
Lieut Col
Comdg 1st S. A. Infy

WAR DIARY
or
INTELLIGENCE SUMMARY.

(Erase heading not required.)

Army Form C. 2118.

Place	Date	Hour	Summary of Events and Information	Remarks and references to Appendices
BOUZINCOURT	22/3/17		Support line. Hostile aircraft over quite active during the day, and appeared to be dropping bombs on rear areas. Casualties - nil.	
- do -	23/3/17		The Battalion relieved the 2nd & 9th S.L.I in the front line. Two patrols left our lines but returned having nothing to report. Enemy artillery was active during the day, but opened up a heavy bombardment of the immediate support line and along the Railway Track at 4.30 p.m. Hostile machine guns were active during the bombardment. Our machine brought down two Enemy planes between 3 and 3.30 p.m. Enemy this morning 2 aero usual patrols had nothing to report. Both artilleries and machine. Casualties nil.	
- do -	24/3/17			
- do -	25/3/17		Patrols had nothing to report. Enemy called up front line and supports during the day. Otherwise quiet. About 15" small 2 M.G. were dropped in front of our line	

9TH (SCOTTISH) DIVISION
SOUTH AFRICAN INFY BDE.

1ST SOUTH AFRICAN INFY REGT
JAN - FEB 1918

To 66 DIV

9TH (SCOTTISH) DIVISION
SOUTH AFRICAN INFY BDE.

9 Div
So. Carolina Bde.
1st Bn. So. Carolina Inf. Reg.
Jan - Feb. 1918

Army Form C. 2118.

WAR DIARY
or
INTELLIGENCE SUMMARY.
(Erase heading not required.)

Place	Date	Hour	Summary of Events and Information	Remarks and references to Appendices
Brigade Reserve	25/1/18		Training 9 to 12.30 pm. Enemy fired few high velocity shells 200 yds E. of camp.	
	26/1/18		Training 9 to 12.30 pm. Building protection against bombs.	
	27/1/18		Battalion relieved 2nd Regt S.A. Infy at front line. Relief completed by 8.30 pm. No casualties. A and C Coys in front line, B in support, D in Garrison in village.	
Left Sub Section Bois de Hangard 29/1/18	28/1/18		Enemy quiet. Slight artillery activity. Enemy aircraft attempted cross our lines but driven back by Anti aircraft and Machine Gun fire. Enemy artillery quiet.	
Sector	29/1/18		Much aerial activity. One aircraft heavily shot on by M.Gs when attempting crossing our lines.	
	30/1/18		Quiet.	
	31/1/18		Quiet. Misty morning.	

P. Prinsloo
Major
Comdg 1st S.A. Infy.

Army Form C. 2118

WAR DIARY
or
INTELLIGENCE SUMMARY
(Erase heading not required.)

Instructions regarding War Diaries and Intelligence Summaries are contained in F. S. Regs., Part II. and the Staff Manual respectively. Title Pages will be prepared in manuscript.

Place	Date	Hour	Summary of Events and Information	Remarks and references to Appendices
Don Camp MOISLAINS	13/1/18		Regiment moved by march route to Moislains	
"	14/1/18		Day devoted to cleaning of equipment and clothing	
"	15/1/18		Training 9AM to 12.30PM	
"	16/1/18		As for 15th inst	
"	17/1/18		As for 15th inst however carried out musketry owing rapid Draft of 39 O.R.s arrived. 184 men employed on various working parties	
"	18/1/18		Training 9am to 12.30pm - 18 O.R.s reinforcements arrived (Durham) draft of 17th O.R.s carried out Training 8.30am to Noon Regt. invited attend concert at VIIth Corps Rest Station at 7pm.	
"	19/1/18			
"	20/1/18		Sunday- Church Parade. No training	
"	21/1/18		Training 9 to 12.30pm. Regt again attended concert at VIIth Corps Rest Station	
"	22/1/18		Training 9 to 12.30 Am - do -	
"	23/1/18			
"	24/1/18		Regt. moved to Reserve billets at L.I. Camp and relieved 10th Argyll & Sutherland Highlanders.	

WAR DIARY
or
INTELLIGENCE SUMMARY

Army Form C. 2118

(Erase heading not required.)

Place	Date	Hour	Summary of Events and Information	Remarks and references to Appendices
Support Line Gonjecourt Sector	8/1/18		Enemy Artillery active, several enemy roaming parties over Batln. HQ. No casualties.	
Front Line Gonjecourt Sector	9/1/18		The Regt relieved 2nd Regt. S.A Infantry in front line. Relief was completed by 8.30 a.m. Snow storm on just before relief commenced. No casualties during relief.	
	10/1/18		Enemy shelled front and support trenches heavily causing two casualties - 1 killed and 1 wounded. Puits dump in rest of day.	
			Enemy artillery fairly active. Sunken road in support shelled. Probably light railway track observed by enemy. Much movement by enemy. Observed in neighbourhood of Gonnelieu. At 10 am a squadron of enemy planes attempted to cross our lines, but were driven off by a squadron of our machines. At 11.15 am and 12.10 am enemy attempts crossing our lines but were driven off by Anti aircraft fire.	
	11/1/18		Our artillery carried out 15 minutes bombardment of enemy trenches commencing at 6.17 am. Slight reply from enemy.	
	12/1/18		Quiet day. Battalion relieved in front line by 9th Rl Regt Scots and 9th Sco. Rifles. jun. Relief completed without any casualties. Regt moved to billets	

WAR DIARY or INTELLIGENCE SUMMARY

Army Form C. 2118

13 A Suply Bn

Place	Date	Hour	Summary of Events and Information	Remarks and references to Appendices
Front Line	1/1/18		Enemy very quiet. Much recce work observed & especially wiring	
GOUZEAUCOURT Sector	2/1/18		Enemy shelled front and support lines about 9.30am and 2pm. Enemy fairly active with M.Gs. Much recce work. Our front Hostile aircraft patrolled our own lines all day.	
	3/1/18		Enemy artillery busy during morning. Quiet in afternoon. Casualties 1 killed and two wounded. Visibility good & many small parties of enemy seen carrying timber &c.	
	4/1/18		Enemy again fairly active during morning. No M.Gs. Support lines shelled. Patrols of men without equipment were seen carrying wood &c from GONNELIEU. Regt was relieved by 2nd Regt S.A. Infantry and moved to support lines. Relief completed by 2.30 am without casualties.	
Support Lines Gouzeaucourt Sector	5/1/18		Enemy but very little over Regt supports doing no damage. Nothing to report.	
	6/1/18		Enemy again shelled supports and caused some slight casualties. Nothing to report. A few 105 mm shells fell near supports at various times during day. No casualties. Evidently searching for our gun positions	
	7/1/18			

WAR DIARY
or
INTELLIGENCE SUMMARY.

Army Form C. 2118.

1 SA Inf Bn
JB 23
6

Place	Date	Hour	Summary of Events and Information	Remarks and references to Appendices
G.H.Q. Rwd	1/2/18		The Battn. was relieved on night 31/1st by 1/1st. Cambridgeshire Regt. Relief completed by 10 pm. Battn. entrained at siding near Fins in two trains (Becourville) and proceeded to Peronne - arriving after midnight & encamped in field. Battn. entrained at Peronne - Flamecourt Stn. at 9 am on 1st and proceeded to Fe Plateau. Detrained and marched to Billets outside Cappy arriving at 1 pm	
Cappy	2/2/18		Day spent in cleaning up.	
	3/2/18		Sunday - Church Services all denominations	
	4/2/18		Training 9-12.30 pm	
	5/2/18		Training 8.30 pm to 12.30 pm	
	6/2/18		Training 8.30-12.30 pm. Soccer football match played against S.A.M.C. Result 3-nil in favour of S.A.M.C.	
	7/2/18		Training 8.30 - 12.30 pm	
	8/2/18		- do -	
	9/2/18		- do -	
	10/2/18		Sunday Church services all denominations. Played Rugby football match against S.A.M.C. Result 53-nil against same.	

WAR DIARY or INTELLIGENCE SUMMARY

Army Form C. 2118

Place	Date	Hour	Summary of Events and Information	Remarks and references to Appendices
G.H.Q. RJM Cappy.	11/2/18		A. & B. Coys proceeded to rifle range at FOUCAUCOURT for Musketry training. C & D Coys. Reveille 8.30 - 12.30. Race Pari. C & D Coys. Reveille – C. Coy. 1st. 3 pm Reveille	
	12/2/18		Training 8.30 – 12.30 pm. Reveille Race – A & B. Coys Reveille A. Coy 1st.	
	13/2/18		Training 8.30 am & 12.30 pm. C & D Coys on range at FOUCAUCOURT for day's Musketry. Rugby match 1st Rouen Picken Coy 1st v 3rd Regt Result 15L nil in favour 1st Regt.	
	14/2/18		Training 8.30 am – 12.30 pm. Sigrs & Transport firing on range.	
	15/2/18		8.30 am – 12.30 pm. 7 Off; 110 men transferred to 1st Regt from 3rd Regt on reorganisation of I.A. Bn. Draft of 7 Off; 176 O/Ranks (Bolsheviks) arrived from Base.	
	16/2/18		Training 8.30 am to 12.30 pm. Rugby match 1st vs 4th Regt 2nd round Liken Coup. Result 11 nil in favour of 1st Regt.	
	17/2/18		Sunday – Bath – marched to Belin-Au-Wood and to attend memorial service at 1 pm. A.B.C. & D. Coys: Less draft proceeded to Ebry-sur-Somme for work on railway. Hqrs remained at Cappy.	

WAR DIARY or INTELLIGENCE SUMMARY

Army Form C. 2118

Place	Date	Hour	Summary of Events and Information	Remarks and references to Appendices
S.H.Q. Res. CAPPY	18/2/18		Training for draft 8.30 - 9/12.30 pm	
	19/2/18		- do -	
	20/2/18		- do -	
	21/2/18		Training 8.30 - 12.30.	
	22/2/18		Training 8.30 to 12 noon. Final Rugby 1st vs 2nd Regt. Result 29 - nil in favour of 1st Regt. 1st Regt. win cup now in possession of 1st Regt for 2nd time.	
	23/2/18		Team who played in yesterday's match granted permission to visit Amiens. Training 8.30 to 12.30 pm. Draft of 84 ORs arrive 7.30 pm.	
	24/2/18		Sunday. Church Services all denominations.	
	25/2/18		Training 8.30 - 12.30	
	26/2/18		Brigade tactical scheme. Baths moved off at 8.15 am A, B, C, and D. Coys returned from working party at CLERY	
	27/2/18		Training 8.30 am to 12.30 pm.	
	28/2/18		Training 8.30 am to 12.30 am. Rugby Football 1st vs 3rd Tank Bn. Result 33 - nil in favour First Regt.	

www.ingramcontent.com/pod-product-compliance
Lightning Source LLC
Chambersburg PA
CBHW051527190426
43193CB00045BA/2183